BULLETS,
BADGES,
AND
BRIDLES

D1563993

BULLETS, BADGES, AND BRIDLES

Horse Thieves and the Societies That Pursued Them

JOHN K. BURCHILL

PELICAN PUBLISHING COMPANY
Gretna 2014

The word "Pelican" and the depiction of a pelican are
trademarks of Pelican Publishing Company, Inc., and are
registered in the U.S. Patent and Trademark Office.

ISBN: 9781455618576
E-book ISBN: 9781455618583

Printed in the United States of America

Published by Pelican Publishing Company, Inc.
1000 Burmaster Street, Gretna, Louisiana 70053

Table of Contents

Acknowledgements

As a non-historian I find myself in debt to many as I pursued this venture. Kate Wise was always willing to take time from her campus librarian role to assist me in my search for obscure titles. Several other libraries and librarians were very helpful including the City of Salina Public Library and the Campbell Room—"my off campus office;" the Kansas Historical Association and its many employees and volunteers working the call desk, who often proved to be better researchers on the topic than myself; Gwenith Podeschi of the Abraham Lincoln Presidential library; Ben Terwilliger and the Eudora Historical Society; and the staff of the Indiana Historical Society all proved very helpful. Ron Brogan and Felix Diskin of the Osage Mission-Neosho County Museum treated me like royalty in my pursuit of information on the Anti Horse-Thief Association and W.W. Graves. Thanks to two students: Amanda Wilkinson and Shawn Chesterman, who were sent in pursuit of historical horse thieves always wondering if their professor "lost it." A very special recognition needs to be given to Kansas Wesleyan University for allowing me time to chase historical horse thieves, my colleagues in the Behavioral Science Department, Dr. Don Olsen, mentor and friend; Dr. Anita Specht, a historian with great patience with non-historians; and Professor Diane Wayman for her patient tutoring in style and syntax. Last, but by no mean least, I wish to thank my wife Susan, daughter Bea, and son Baxter who already is a much better author than his old man.

Introduction

Indeed, history is nothing more than a tableau of crimes and misfortunes.

—Voltaire

I pursued the topic of horse thieves and anti-horse thief societies, when time allowed, out of personal interest with a focus on the local history of anti-horse thief associations. I thought about delving more in depth into the topic and found the excuse of not having an academic background in history (I teach criminal justice) to quell most desires to pursue more serious research. I also had no desire to create an academic tome that would appeal to a very narrow audience. All this was ruined when the chair of the English department asked if I would consider teaching a one-time American crime fiction course. This idea intrigued me, requiring that I step outside my academic realm into one that I have supported for my whole adult life.

In reading *The Cambridge Companion to American Crime Fiction* edited by Catherine Ross Nickerson, one passage struck me as being just as applicable to anti-horse thief societies as crime fiction and bolstered my passion to pursue this topic for it is really in the bailiwick of the generalist—a study of culture, history and criminal justice.

When we study detective fiction [anti-horse thief societies], we can think broadly and deeply about American history

9

and culture. When we are looking at stories about deviants in conflict with the agents of law and order, we are looking straight into the workings of society. The villains and heroes of popular literature [horse theft] are very instructive; they tell us about what we fear and who we would conjure up to contain what threatens us. They reveal our racial and religious prejudices and our gender biases. . . . [anti-horse thief societies] developed . . . in the middle of the nineteenth century, a period shaped by the tumultuous forces of urbanization, social stratification, geographical mobility and changing gender roles.[1]

Therefore a study and understanding of horse thieves and the formation and operation of anti-horse-thief societies must be done not just in a historical context but in the cultural and geographic landscape of social control and deviance. Examining the various responses to horse theft adds not just to our understanding of crime and punishment but also to the role citizen organizations, such as the anti-horse-thief societies, have played in the public versus private enforcement of values, morals, and laws.

From the frontier settlements in Jamestown to the boom towns of the old west, each society had norms or rules that set expectations of behavior that were codified in compacts or laws or understood as the code of conduct. Many of these early compacts were the creation of self-protection societies, including the protection from horse theft. The mores—those norms that have great moral significance and are commonly held—included "the sanctity of womanhood and the home," "private property," and "Thou shall not steal." These and many others were enforced, from time to time, by anti-horse-thief societies.

Cultural values of the United States have always included property, freedom, locomotion, and fair play. The horse was central to them all. The horse was invaluable for clearing the land, planting, and harvesting crops, and it represented a substantial financial investment. The mobility, freedom, and status represented by the horse can be easily understood in modern terms by looking at the cultural obsession with the automobile. The make, model, and car/truck/SUV choices all place a premium on "you are what you drive." In addition to the implied status that a car embodies, it also represents freedom, independence, and a substantial investment to the point that one can see movement to enhance "make my day laws" to allow the use of force to prevent car theft/carjacking, in addition to home invasions.

In studying the concept of horse thefts and the corresponding response, one must determine the extent and nature of the crime. The void of consistent crime reporting in colonial America, expansion of the formal criminal justice system in the Old West, and the plethora of small compact/covenant groups to respond to horse thefts resulted in a "dark figure of crime" that shrouded an accurate assessment of the extent and nature of the problem. This was only made worse by the fact that many of the criminal gangs and the anti-horse-thief associations were secret/private and the crimes of members, and the organizations' responses, often were never reported—staying in the shadows.

As the nation became more "civilized," society transitioned from personal enforcement of law to communal enforcement and then, procedurally, to the centralized actions of the government. Technological advances in communication and transportation made law enforcement more effective and the anti-horse-thief society has become nothing more than a social group.

The first chapter of this book explores the birth of anti-horse-thief societies. During the colonial era, covenant groups and formal compacts first begin to address the detection, apprehension, and often punishment of horse thieves. The pattern of increased horse theft after wars established in this era, as is the response that created the early anti-horse-thief societies. As one society noted: "The founders of the Pownal (Vt.) Association to Counteract and Detect Horse Thieves cited 'the pernicious practise of horsestealing.' Which had recently 'become so prevalent and repeatedly practised' in their town as their reason for establishing a society in 1789."[2]

Chapter two explores the various tricks of the trade used by horse thieves and those who pursued them. The *modus operandi* of the various professional horse thieves is explored. As the populace moved west, the void of effective police protection led people to organize voluntary associations to combat horse theft. Not unlike the early societies that were created in the late 1700s in New England, members were required to keep descriptions of their horses on file and agree to a mutual pledge system that required members to pursue and apprehend thieves and to return stolen stock.

The early societies and their development in response to horse theft are explored in chapter three. The Civil War created a huge demand for horses and a corresponding increase in horse theft. This period is the heyday of the anti-horse-thief societies, who often had legal authority to carry out their missions, just like their colonial forefathers, of the detection, recovery, and apprehension of horse thieves.

Chapter four examines the issue of vigilantism as a response to horse theft. Some committees of vigilance were appointed; some grew organically. Both vigilante committees and anti-horse-thief societies, on occasion, would make arrests and use violence. When, then, is an anti-horse-thief group a pro social response, sanctioned by the state? When should it be considered an extra-legal response? What social/political/geographical factors would need to be in place to result in the often harsh necktie—meaning hanging—parties? These questions are not easy to answer in a broad brush stroke, with so many shades and details in the portrait of anti-horse-theft societies.

Chapter five is a profile of several horse thieves from the period and location known as the Old West. Some of the thieves started life as law men, slaves, merchants, and soldiers, encompassing men and women from all walks of life. Their stories provide a glimpse into the complex lives of those who chose to commit one of the most serious crimes of the frontier. Chapter six profiles the men who pursued the horse thief. Often the line between the lawman and the thief was blurred, but the profiles help bring into focus the response demanded by the citizens of the western expansion.

Chapter seven is an examination of the birth of the Anti-Horse Thief Association, the largest interstate anti-horse-thief society in the United States. The A.H.T.A. or, "Antis" as they referred to themselves, were birthed in Missouri in 1854. It quickly grew with many chapters throughout the Midwest and plains states including Arkansas, Illinois, Iowa, Kansas, Oklahoma Indian Territory, and Nebraska. With the motto "Protect the innocent; bring the guilty to justice" this fraternal organization kept active well into the twentieth century.

Chapter eight follows the growth of the Anti-Horse Thief Association to one of the largest fraternal organizations whose focus was on crime prevention and intervention. The organization's growth included an intelligence arm and briefing book, a weekly newspaper, the creation of an auxiliary unit for women, and a reputation that led them to be called upon to fight many other crimes than just horse theft. The chapter also follows the demise of the A.H.T.A. through two world wars, the increase of effective communication systems, the infiltration by another secret society, and the replacement of the horse with the automobile.

This book ends with several appendices that are intended to give the reader a closer look at the structure, organization, and minds of the early societies. Independent and local societies as well as examples of interstate organizations are included. These should be read in the context of the time period and location of the organizations, although many similarities will become apparent.

From the introduction of the modern horse in Egypt

around 1750 B.C. to its use as an instrument of warfare by Cortez in 1519, the horse has played an important role in the culture and geography of man. In the Americas, the horse became pivotal in the cultural landscape and expansion of the New World. Let us explore the rich history and culture of horse theft and the various societies created to detect, apprehend, and return horses to their rightful owners.

Saddle up!

Chapter 1

The Birth of Anti-Horse Thief Societies

In the period of United States history known as the colonial era (late 1500s to early 1800s), crime was not a major focus of concern—basic survival was. The majority of the average American Colonial's day was spent in basic survival activities: hunting, gathering, and planting food; collecting water and firewood; and building and improving on their homes, barns, and other outbuildings. Neighbors were more than the people who lived next door; they were fellow pioneers who shared the same dreams and aspirations, weaving a web of reliance that included trapping the occasional horse thief.

Most of the colonists lived in small communities, which meant that the detection of a crime, and often the person responsible, was not easy to evade. A crime committed by someone outside the community, a stranger, often would increase the fear associated with crime. Horse theft, as a crime in general, often included removing the animal from the area to be used or sold without fear of being discovered. Given the typical *modus operandi* of this crime, therefore, apprehension required pursuit, if the animal was to be recovered. Fear of the often unknown thief, the direction of travel, and the many possible outcomes in a confrontation, required several people, a society, be involved in responding to the crime. And this method of response was familiar to many.

Colonial cities often required their residents to serve in various organizations and societies for the mutual protection of life and property. In 1712, Philadelphia imposed a fine on any adult male who refused to serve as a member of the watch. In Charleston, South Carolina, local law created a night watch that consisted of constables and local citizens who would serve on a regular rotating basis. Heads of households, male or female, were pressed into service, and a fine awaited any who missed a rotation unless he provided an appropriate substitute. The watch, who were authorized to arrest any wrongdoer, worked a shift that lasted from ten in the evening until sunrise.

The early American militia system is a classic example of the citizen role in community safety. In Boston, from 1760 to 1820, more than 1,900 voluntary associations were created. By the 1820s at least seventy a year were founded. These associations were diverse in make-up and purpose, but they did include associations for the enforcement of laws, including associations specifically formed for the detection and apprehension of horse thieves. This phenomenon was not limited to Boston or Massachusetts. The idea of citizen organizations to prevent and combat crime is well ingrained in early American culture. Societies for the detection and apprehension of horse thieves are a natural and pragmatic extension of this culture.

Capt. William Lynch was proud of what he had built out of the wilderness now known as Virginia. It had not been easy. Weather was much more wild and unpredictable than the old country. Clearing land for the planting of crops was backbreaking work whose monotony was interrupted only by assisting his neighbors in a barn raising or harvest. It felt good to, on occasion, stand back and look at what he had accomplished. These reflections were brief, for taming the beast of nature required constant attention else it would revert to its wild nature.

Lynch did not mind helping his neighbors on occasion. He understood that these breaks in the realization of his own dreams created an unwritten *quid pro quo* where he could count on assistance in return. Lynch knew and relied upon the character of his neighbors. A man's character was often the only currency that he had to trade. The social cohesion created by neighbor helping neighbor was often the one factor that kept a man's dreams from turning into a nightmare.

The one call for assistance that really upset Lynch was a call from neighbors to respond to a crime. If a man's horse was stolen, or his neighbor's horse, he was rightfully indignant. Time must be spent away from planting or harvest to investigate and attempt to gain the stolen animal back. Responding to a common enemy brings people together, but in colonial America it meant time away from survival—time away from fulfilling one's dreams. Lynch had had enough. The wide geographical boundaries and lack of a centralized government meant that any help had to come from Lynch and his neighbors.

Lynch met with his neighbors in Pittsylvania County, Virginia, in 1780 and they agreed to band together to protect themselves from horse thieves and other criminals. Set forth in writing, this became one of the earliest societies created to fight horse thieves, spurring many others to follow suit.

> Whereas, many of the inhabitants of the county of Pittsylvania . . . have sustained great and intolerable losses by a set of lawless men . . . that . . . we, the subscribers, being determined to put a stop to the iniquitous practices of those unlawful and abandoned wretches, do enter into the following association . . . and if they will not desist from their evil practices, we will inflict such corporeal punishment on him or them, as to us shall seem adequate to the crime committed or the damage sustained.
>
> —William Lynch et al., Agreement, 1780

Captain Lynch was not the only "Lynch" Virginian. At about the same time a Virginia planter, Col. Charles Lynch, who served as a colonel under Gen. Nathanael Greene during the revolutionary war, and his fellow planters formed an organization with the expressed purpose to punish *horse thieves* and any other criminals. Suspects, almost always a Tory (pro-England), would be arrested and brought to the home of Lynch. A trial would be held with three neighbors acting as associate justices, and the accused was allowed to present witnesses and plead his case. If he was condemned, the punishment would range from whipping to hanging. Those found innocent would receive an apology and sometimes even reparations.[1] Between the vigorous actions of both Lynches against horse thieves and other criminals, "Lynch Law" and "Lynching" quickly entered the American lexicon, forever associated with the fate of horse thieves.

The majority of vigilant societies that were formed in the colonial era were started by farmers to address the crime of horse theft. The earliest society seems to have been formed in Northampton, Massachusetts, in 1782, one year before the formal end of the Revolutionary War. The horse's importance in war made it a prime target for thieves operating black markets selling to both the British and revolutionaries. The Revolutionary War gave the colonists freedom from British rule and taught the population that much could be accomplished through collective action. Just as the founding fathers met to form a new nation and sign their intent through a Declaration of Independence, this era saw the start of covenant groups and formal compacts to address the detection, apprehension, and often punishment of horse thieves. In 1786 the Friends of Justice was born in Wilmington, Delaware. "The primary objective of the earliest vigilants was the horse; hence, the label *horse-thief societies.*"[2] In 1789 the Pownal Association to Counteract and Detect Horse Thieves was created when horse theft was so rampant in their community that collective action was seen as the only resort.

How anti-horse-thief societies persecuted the offenders was divided between turning them over to the centralized legal system and acting as their own judge and jury. In many areas of the colonies, the victim would be expected to pay the expenses of prosecution. Taken in conjunction with the time and costs associated with leaving their farms and businesses, traveling to the nearest court, and returning to give testimony in court, often summary judgment made much more sense from a fiscal perspective.

Whatever their response, these early societies made their objective clear with their names:

1782	MA	Northampton Society for the Detection of Thieves and Robbers
1786	DE	Friends of Justice
1789	VT	Pownal Association to Counteract and Detect Horse Thievery
1791	MA	Oxford Society for the Detection of Horsestealers and Thieves
1793	CT	Woodstock Theft Detection Society
1795	MA	Massachusetts Society for Detecting Horse Thieves
1795	MA	Society for Detecting Horse Thieves in the Towns of Mendon, Bellingham, and Milford
1796	CT	Glastonbury Association for the Detecting Horse Thieves
1796	MA	Rehoboth, Seekonk and Pawtucket Detecting Society
1797	MA	Norton Detecting Society Formed for the Purpose of Detecting Horse Thieves and Recovering Horses

The swift and sure capture, and sometime lynching, of a horse thief provided both specific and general deterrence. Specific deterrence was aimed at ensuring that the individual offender does not repeat his crime. Jail, public whippings, branding, mutilation, restitution, and public shaming were efforts by communities to invoke individual rehabilitation. General deterrence was accomplished through harsh punishments that sent a message to all potential horse thieves not to consider similar actions. Although these rules might have worked within a given community, the colonials had to face the ongoing problem of horse theft from Native Americans and as a result of war.

Native Americans and the Horse

The speed of the integration of the horse into Native American culture is something akin to an anthropological breaking of the sound barrier. Prior to 1541, Spanish law expressly prohibited any Native American from riding a horse. Facing a revolt in central Mexico, the viceroy of New Spain realized that he needed the help and support of Aztec chieftains so he gave them horses—creating the first recorded evidence of the new relationship between the horse and Native Americans.[3]

Prior to the introduction of horses in the United States, Native Americans traveled by foot or along water routes in canoes. To many Native American tribes the horse was a strange new animal seen as a food source rather than an indispensable tool. The strangeness quickly wore off and the value quickly came into focus. The Navajo Apaches located to the northwest of early European settlements were known to steal horses as early as 1659. Historian Haines (1938) reported that: "Five years later an account states that this has become a constant practice, and that the Apaches to the east bring in Indian captives from other tribes to trade for horses."

By the mid-eighteenth century horses had become an integral cultural component of the Native Americans between the Great Lakes and the Ohio River. The horses were obtained through trade and war parties. Horse theft from the British and colonists became another common source for horse flesh. This was a "serious problem" at Fort Pitt along the Ohio River:

> On July 10, 1761, Colonel Henry Bouquet, a British Officer, cut off all trade with the Shawnees until they promised to stop stealing horses and returned the white prisoners being held. In later years Johnson complained that the Indians were stealing horses from both the British government and the traders.[4]

Bouquet also pointed out that pack horses and draft horses were not only numerous but important to Fort Pitt and the frontier outpost. The trip over the mountains was arduous not just to the travelers, but to the horses as well. The norm was to turn the horses loose to allow them to graze and recuperate from the trip. In correspondence written on May 4, 1761, Bouquet explained that these horses "were a great temptation to the Indians, who stole them. It was tantalizing and difficult to deal with the horse thief—an individual so ubiquitous on the frontier."[5]

There were three common root causes of the theft of horses by the Native Americans. The first cause is the constant and often-organized war against the various Native American tribes. From the introduction of the horse in 1519 through the turn of the twentieth century, there were ongoing hostilities between the white settlers and the indigenous peoples. Horses were an integral instrument of war in the ongoing struggles. The second cause was the utilitarian nature of the horse. Prior to the horse, dogs were the only pack animals used by Native Americans but they adapted to horses easily: "As they already developed techniques for handling dogs, the natives found it relatively easy to transfer that experience. Indeed, for many Plains tribes, horses were thought of as a larger, more useful breed of dog."[6]

The ability to increase transportation and hunting with a horse fit the culture of so many of the Native Americans that by the mid-1700s the horse had spread to many tribes including those of the Plains. Many Native Americans captured wild horses, but with the blatant discrimination and social disadvantages faced by so many Native Americans, theft could be rationalized as a viable option to obtain what could not be owned through conformity to the societal norms. The third cause was the value placed on horses after the rapid acculturation of this animal. It did not take long before the horse became the symbol of wealth. In an effort to accumulate more horses, and the corresponding social standing, raiding parties between rival tribes became common. This method of accumulating status in a community through the amount or breed of horses was similarly mirrored in many of the European settled communities.

> My horse be swift in flight.
> Even like a bird;
> My horse be swift in flight.
> Bear me now in safety
> far from enemy arrows,
> And you shall be rewarded
> With streamers and ribbons red.
>
> —*Sioux Warrior's Song*[7]
> (Whitelaw 2007, 118)

In the land that was to become Kansas, the Pawnee culture not only changed to assimilate the horse but also manipulated their environment to support the horse. The Pawnees had discovered that by setting fire to the dead grass in the spring, the green-up period was hastened for the purpose of grazing of their horses.[8] If the Native Americans were quick to adopt the horse into their culture, the same could be said for the cowboy and the Cossack—both of whom had to keep vigilant against the horse thief.

Cowboys & Cossacks

On the other side of the world, the legend of man and

horse continued in the form of the Russian Cossack. These superb cavalry members personified much the same mythos as the American cowboy. Protecting the borders and justice of mother Russia from the saddle, they provided just as many stories and legends to the people of Russia as the American cowboy. For both the cowboy and Cossack, for both the farmer/rancher and peasant, the importance of the horse cannot be overestimated. To look into horse theft and the peasant response in Russia in the 1880s is to look in a mirror of the American experience. Consider the following story from Russia in the mid-1880s:

> Gritsenko immediately recognized the man as an inveterate horse thief suspected of several crimes in his village, including the theft of one hundred rubles from Gritsenko himself. The elder physically overpowered the thief and then tied him up with his belt. He swung his victim across his back and carried him back to Potasha repeatedly shouting to villagers, "*Hromada* [assembly of heads of the household], to the meeting place, Nen'ka has been caught."[9]

The villagers held a quick "trial" where Nen'ka confessed and named several accomplices who were summoned before the assembly, pled guilty, and were jailed. After several bottles of courage, the assembly returned to the jail, removed the guilty parties, and the beatings began (one of the horse thieves died from his injuries). Though this occurred in Imperial Russia, this just as easy could be an event from Caldwell, Kansas. The theft of horses was just as important in peasant life of the late Imperial Russia as it was for the settlers of the western states.

The incidence of horse theft and the responses to it were a matter of the demographics of the frontier settler, geography of the new lands, as well as the political landscape. The self-sufficient and independent nature of those living in the frontier was one that would not wait for the lag of government-run law enforcement to catch up with the spreading population.

As Christine D. Worobeck (1987) pointed out, in the United States, as well as Russia, "The incidence of theft [horse] and background of the thieves, the limitations of government response, and above all the reactions of peasants themselves reveal much about rural conditions and outlook, and particularly the balance between state and self-government among Russia's [and the United States] majority."

In Russia as well as the United States, horse thieves could be found operating in gangs with their own networks to identify potential victims and markets for the stolen horses. Horses would be stolen in one area and sold in another to avoid detection. Consider the Talbott Gang that operated out of the southwest part of the Oklahoma Indian Territory in the early 1880s. This gang was one of many that used the Oklahoma Indian Territory as a base, in part, because of the jurisdictional headaches it caused those in pursuit, and the geography seemed to be created with the idea of hiding stolen horses and cattle.[10] Horses stolen in Missouri and Kansas could be hidden in the canyons and caves of the Oklahoma Indian Territory and sold to unsuspecting buyers in Colorado.

Historically, the idea of using state jurisdictional lines to confound pursuit was not a new development in the United States. In the late 1700s in New England "Thirty-three societies were located near state lines, where they served victims of theft who wished to recover stolen goods without engaging the vexations process of extradition. Indeed, thieves recognized that jurisdictional questions could impede the public authorities, and they often planned their operations accordingly."[11] In 1902 there were 219 chapters of the Anti-Horse Thief Association located in Kansas. One hundred and fifty of the chapters were located in fourteen of the counties that bordered Missouri and the Oklahoma Indian Territory with 6,127 members on the rolls. This excludes similar organizations such as the Central Protective Association.

Across the globe, geography also came into play when

stolen horses were hidden in canyons and caves. "The village of Zbeliutka was an ideal headquarters for the thieves because it had a large underground cavern . . . a rendezvous point for stolen horses before they were whisked away across the border to be sold."[12] This bears more than a striking similarity to Mitchell County, Iowa. "Stolen horses were hidden in a cave on the west bank of the Cedar River . . . concealed until the search was disbanded, and then taken out of the country."[13] With little or lax enforcement by the government along the Russian frontier, the various communities engaged in extralegal action to detect, apprehend, and punish horse thieves. Punishment included hanging, beatings, branding, torture, and even banishment.

The responses of the peasants in post-emancipation Russia (the 1880s) to horse thievery showcased the inability of the centralized government to effectively deal with the issue, not unlike what was occurring in the Old West. The horse was too valuable to be lost to theft. The time needed to track down and return stolen horses made it difficult for a farmer to drop his work and chase the outlaws. The Russian peasants went after horse thieves with the same collective action, the same purpose, as was seen in the United States. Their survival depended upon cooperation of neighbors and friends in not just agricultural tasks, but in the detection and apprehension of criminals. The American cowboys and the Cossacks made their living astride a horse in the 1880s and witnessed the same struggles and responses to the crime of horse theft on the frontier.

Indians, Gypsies & Horse Thieves

Violence, particularly vigilante violence, is much easier to commit against people who are demonized by the actors of the violence. Two groups have been strongly demonized by the white European settlers in general, and regarding horse theft in particular: Native Americans and Gypsys. The Native Americans long held the role of scapegoat for all manner of thievery, deserved or not. In the Yellowstone area, white settlers agreed that "the Absaroka (Crow) were inveterate and skillful thieves. Men, women, and children were adept at pilfering and the only disgrace connected with it was to get caught at it."[14] On the other hand, a white man stealing horses from a Native American was not considered a crime; it was more along the lines of good fortune.

Keeping the Native Americans a marginalized people made it easier for vigilantes to mete out justice. In May 1853 in the San Fernando Valley, Native Americans stole some horses that belonged to the area Indian Agent. The "noble sentiments" of those who gave pursuit were described by one of the riders:

> We will let those rascally redskins know that they have no longer to deal with the Spaniard or the Mexican, but with the invincible race of American backwoodsmen, which has driven the savage from Plymouth Rock to the Rocky Mountains, and has headed him off here on the western shore of the continent, and will drive him back to meet his kindred fleeing westward, all to be drowned in the great Salt Lake.[15]

As this sentiment demonstrates, not just the Native American was marginalized but the Spanish and Mexican, also, foreshadowing the groups to follow, such as the anti-Catholic, Chinese, and union "leagues."

It wasn't always just stealing a horse that would get a thief into trouble, but whom the horse was stolen from. Discrimination and the demonization of the Native American was much too common in the old west. Steal a white man's horse and you could be hung; steal the horse from a Native American and you would not be given a second thought. It was this attitude that almost saved Billy Downs and California Ed. Billy Downs had garnered a reputation of stealing horses and feasting on beef with dubious origins. One year on July 4, the Montana vigilantes ordered Billy Downs and California Ed from their home to answer charges of stealing horses and killing cattle. Quick to admit to stealing horses from Indians, they held fast to their story of never stealing from white men. Normally this would have resolved itself as a simple misunderstanding, but when the horses in their pens were studied twenty-six of them had the brands of white men. Stealing from white men could not be tolerated so they were quickly taken to a nearby grove, sturdy trees were selected, and Billy Downs and California Ed were hung.

The *Anti-Horse Thief Weekly News* (1902) tells the story of the early days of Topeka, Kansas, when there were three brothers who were known to be the terror of the area. Killing was "their idea of a humorous incident . . . And what was worse in [those] days they stole horses." One of the brothers, Ike, had been drinking when he met Fourchey, a Native American who was also drunk. "They both mounted the Indian's pony, Fourchey in the saddle and 'Ike' riding behind. After a series of blood curdling whoops the pair started toward an Indian village on Blacksmith creek, but reaching the present site of Washburn college, 'Ike' decided that he was too proud to ride with a native American, so he playfully stabbed Fourchey in the heart, rolled him off in the trail and getting in the saddle, as befitted a white man of magnitude, rode back to town and absorbed some more fire water." The fact that a cold-blooded murder could be described as a playful stabbing, by itself, showed the attitude of many early pioneers towards Native Americans.

The Anti-Horse Thief Association accepted Native Americans into their organization, but it still took some convincing as is evidenced in the following story that appeared in the *Anti-Horse Thief Association Weekly News* in 1902:

Our lodge is composed of the best material in the land, in more than one. We are a bunch of men standing as one. This lot of men is composed of full blood Cherokee, half breed, and the white men. We are proud of our union. We use interpreters in the lodge so as to make those understand

who do not talk English. Our Vice-president is a full blood
Indian who talks both languages fluently. Our treasurer is a
full blood who does not speak English. . . . We have not had
any thief to catch since we organized over a year ago but I
can promise one thing sure, if our lodge should strike his trail
we would get him, as a full blood Indian can beat the world
trailing anything.[16]

Another group that had long been blamed for horse
theft was the Gypsies. The caption under an illustration of
Hungarian Gendarmes from the September 2, 1899 issue of
The Graphic—a British weekly newspaper—states that the
Gypsies who live in Hungary are all horse thieves and difficult
to capture. An 1883 article published in the *New York
Times* titled "Horse-Stealing as an Art; An English Gypsy's
Operation in America" tells the story of William Temple, a
full-blooded Gypsy, who left England and in 1866 selected
twenty-five "of his kind wandering about the country" to
create a gang of horse thieves. Each member took one of
six roles in the gang: prospectors, actual workers, runners,
doers, gig-workers, and livery-racket men.

Prospectors had to be able to act and assume the different
disguises of a stock-buyer, horse trainer, doctor, or any
other sort of man who would not garner attention in the
shopping for horses, when in fact he would be attempting
to determine where the most valuable horses were kept,
the security, and escape routes. After the intelligence was
reported to the gang headquarters, the actual workers would
be sent out to remove the horses. Typically young, fearless,
and expert horsemen, the actual workers would soon turn
the horses over to the runners. The runners would take the
horse and ride it some distance to a stock farm owned by
the gang. Stock farms were located in New York, New Jersey,
Pennsylvania, Maryland, and Ohio.

Once a stolen horse arrived at a stock farm the "doers," the
artists of the gang, would set about in a process of altering the

appearance of the horse. Some of the techniques included clipping, dyeing, altering brands, and singeing. Many times the appearance change would be so dramatic that the horse could be sold in the same area from which it was stolen! The gang also had a rule never to steal wagons or harnesses from farming neighborhoods. In cities and large towns the gig-workers and livery-racket men would ply their trade. Gig-workers would watch the homes of leading physicians who would drive alone and leave their horses at the homes of patients, where they would be quickly untied and spirited away by the gig-workers. The champion gig-worker of the gang was known as "Dr. Poles."

Working in the livery-racket meant that one would show up to town well dressed with valuable-looking luggage and spend money freely. They would make many "business" trips in the outlying areas renting rigs, returning as promised, and paying promptly. Once a pattern had been established and trust obtained, the livery-racket man would then hire the best team and rig for a pleasure drive never to return. When the gang was broken with arrests, and reported by the press, Gypsies and horse thieves seemed to be inseparable in the minds of many. Another close association with horse theft was war.

War, What's it Good For?

Of all the scars that war bestows upon man, often it is the scars not seen that have the most lasting impact. At the end of the French and Indian War (1763) many men were released from their militia duties and returned to their homes in Pennsylvania, Virginia, and the Carolinas. The sudden transition to civilian life proved difficult for men "who for years had been accustomed to Murder & Pillage." The veterans of war in the backcountry, being forever hyper-vigilant, found themselves "chusing a life of Idleness . . . form'd ymselves into Gangs, and rang'd over, & laid under Contribution y whole Continent."[17] Horse theft proved to be a crime that offered excitement and profit for those who survived. Consider the case of Winslow Driggers.

Some outlaws were corrupted by the disorder and license that accompanied the Cherokee War. Winslow Driggers, for instance, came from the Peedee area and was probably related to Mark Driggers, a landholder on the little Peedee. As a youth of twenty, Driggers fought in the militia under Captain Alexander McIntosh during the Cherokee War and sometime thereafter became an outlaw. Ten years later, a thorough villain, he returned to the Peedee at the head of a marauding gang.[18]

The story of Winslow Driggers was a very familiar one throughout the history of the United States. The aftermath of war seemed to have brought about waves of expansion and crime. The anti-horse-thief movement arose "spontaneously" after the Revolutionary War. This is easy to understand, for during the Revolutionary War the use of, and corresponding demand for, horses spiked. Redcoats and state militias alike were quick to "release" horses held "captive" by farmers. The Revolutionary War, for many of the colonials, "debased public authority." "After the war [Revolutionary], armed, rootless men drifted home to find few economic opportunities awaiting them. The war also disrupted traditional social hierarchies, making it difficult for local notables to impose order through position."[19] Law and order seemed to apply only to a select and privileged few while the rest experienced a void that the criminal quickly exploited. In 1793 the Woodstock Connecticut Theft Detecting Society was established because "horse stealing had become an occupation."[20] Volunteerism during the war gave the public further skills needed to create anti-horse-thief societies. The number of anti-horse-thief societies exploded throughout New England. As the expansion of the country moved west, a second anti-horse-thief movement "spontaneously" arose at the start of the Civil War, exploding in number by the end of the war.

The Civil War brought a high demand and corresponding high prices for good horses. Both Union and Confederate forces made attempts to legally obtain horses, and when the legitimate sources ran dry, there was a flourishing black market. Many troops engaged in the routine behavior of raiding towns and farms for needed supplies during long and extended campaigns. "Horses had been taken as needed from the beginning. This was the custom of cavalrymen, both Union and Confederate. It not only gave the raiders fresh mounts along the way, it denied them to their pursuers."[21]

As the scarcity of horses increased, so did the actions of the horse thief. In 1861 Kansas, "organized gangs of horse thieves threatened to sweep the boarder clean of livestock." The standard *modus operandi* of these gangs was to reconnoiter border farmers and ranchers, identify those who seemed to be politically indifferent, "accuse him of disloyalty, then despoil him of his wealth. With a good horse going for hundreds of dollars on the black market, the rewards were great."[22]

On September 11, 1856 the Kansas territorial governor, John W. Geary, issued a proclamation to disband all militia and other armed organizations. The fight between anti- and pro-slavers was seen by many victims as acts of terrorism. "The problem of horsestealing is one of more than passing importance in this stage of the story of Kansas and its leaders, although it has been customary to ignore it."[23]

The winter of 1856-57 saw the National Kansas Committee report "during the last war a great deal of damage has been done by the system of pressing horses." Claims to the committee for stolen horses showed that it was a regular practice for followers of John Brown, as well as pro-slavers, to steal horses in Kansas and sell them in Iowa. The money gained would then be used to purchase guns to aid the continuation of the fight that garnered the title "Bloody Kansas." An editorial in the June 20, 1857 edition of the *Herald of Freedom* titled "Be on the Lookout" explained it thus:

Reader, would you know who were concerned in stealing and running off horses to Iowa last summer and autumn; and who opposed the pacific efforts of Gov. Geary to restore tranquility to this distracted territory? Would you know who it is that is desirous for another collision; and who, as soon as the strife should open would be seen on some honest man's horse making all possible speed to Iowa again that he might sell the horse, and return for another. Go into the street at any time of day in Lawrence, and you will find him denouncing the Herald of Freedom, threatening to read the editor out of the Free State Party, and branding him with being a renegade to the cause of freedom.

For the last week we have been writing down the names of a number of young men of the character given above. Persons visiting Lawrence will have no occasion to see a list of those names; but if the same policy is pursued in the future that has been in the past, our forty-two thousand readers in the East shall have the pleasure of seeing those names, to the end that they can see whether they recognize any old acquaintances. The persons to whom we allude will be particularly bitter during the next few weeks, mark that, and among that number is one reporter for the Eastern press, whose pen has dipped in gall for several months whenever he alluded to our paper.[24]

As Szymanski (2005) pointed out, the surge in anti-horse-thief societies after the Civil War was primarily a western phenomenon and as a result "antitheft societies, along with other regional associations, declined more in the urban Northeast than in other, more rural, parts of the country." The most likely reason for the decline cited was the corresponding increase in police forces in the smaller cities and towns. Following the Civil War there was widespread distrust of law enforcement in the western frontier. Many saw the boom towns as a feudal system, where the landed gentry who did not serve in the war saw the law as a device that applied to others and had the law enforcement officers in their pocket. "That the Civil War was followed by a renewed outbreak of crime throughout the country is a well documented fact."[25] The spike in horse theft in post-war Kansas, Missouri, and Oklahoma often was committed by war veterans. Post war saw gangs made up of ex-guerrillas from both Union and Confederate troops pillaging and seeking revenge for wartime acts and battles won and lost. In Missouri:

Numerous armed bands, each protecting its own interests, clashed in the countryside. Legal protection was often unavailable. All this was not merely the last gasp of the Lost Cause; it was not a simple reflection of Union/Confederate divisions. Many local ex-Confederates, for example, opposed the James-Younger gang. The Confederate background of the outlaws certainly won them some sympathy, but only within the local context of chaotic, factional disorder.[26]

The result was the creation of several vigilante and self-protection groups, including anti-horse-thief societies.

Study any country that has been embroiled in war and it is apparent that destruction is often not limited to lives and property but spreads to the very fabric of the country's social institutions. "The young men who returned from the four-year struggle had come of age while in the service, and regulations accepted as a matter of course by the youths of 1861 were challenged by the veterans of 1865."[27] Attempts to reestablish law and order, to repair the tear in the fabric caused by the war took many forms, such as the temperance movement and the various manifestations of anti-horse-thief societies. These societies offered the returning men an organization formed along military lines with members who shared similar experiences, and the ability to ensure some control in the reestablishment of law and order in their communities.

Chapter 2

Tricks of the Thieves and Pursuers

History is filled with stories of the thieves who specialized in horse theft. One of the most infamous colonial-era horse thieves was George White. George White gained his reputation through cunning and bravado. Often he would steal a horse and take it to another town where he would sell it. After a few hours would pass, White would then steal it from the new and unsuspecting owner, and it would be sold in the next town. It was reported he would then occasionally steal the horse a third time and return it to the pasture of origin before it was ever missed![1] As the history of the country moved forward so did the cunning and organization of the horse thief and horse-thief gangs.

To break up many of the horse-thief gangs required an organized and trained force: one that was able not just to track the outlaws but also to understand how they operated. The seminal work on this topic was written by W.W. Graves in 1905 and was titled *Tricks of Rascals*. Graves had been active in the Anti-Horse Thief Association serving as president of the national order, publisher of the *Anti-Horse Thief Weekly News*, and served in a variety of capacities in the A.H.T.A. locally and nationally. The first "rascal" described is the spotter. The spotter is one who works for horse thieves as a sort of advance scout. The spotter typically assumes the role of one considering the purchase of a horse or farm but never completes the purchase—he always leaves with the admonishment that he needs to consider the deal but never returns. The real purpose of the spotter is to identify stock (potential targets) and create a map of the area including any security concerns. The spotter never steals a horse but does get a share in the proceeds of any successful theft. It is difficult to identify the spotter because there may be several days or weeks between his visit and the theft. "His work is so well done that it is almost impossible to apply the law to him even when the real thief is captured. The spotter is really an accessory to the crime, but to prove him such is where the difficulty lies."[2] Collecting and sharing reports between law enforcement agencies and anti-horse-thief societies became very important to apprehend these types of rascals.

The second trick of rascals Graves detailed was relay stations. In the legitimate use of the system, people riding horseback such as the pony express or stage coaches would stop at a relay station and exchange their horse(s) for fresh mounts and continue their journey. For the horse thief, the relay station was used to exchange riders, not horses. A person who stole a horse could ride it to a station where another mounted the animal and continued the journey. This process continued through a number of stations that might extend well into another jurisdiction. Meanwhile the original thief would return quickly to his home where he was seen and no connection was made between him and the horse. Sometimes the original thief would volunteer to help hunt down the thief!

This method was used for the theft of all types of livestock. "The outlaws who came and went from the Hole in the wall . . . would split up into small groups, each taking charge of a few cattle which they would drive to a rendezvous. The next day they would continue on to another small isolated ranch, or 'station,' subsidized by the gang, where the cattle could be held until they were sold."[3] Graves points out that it is not uncommon to find respected members of the community who are keepers of these stations of stolen livestock.

Once stolen, if the horse was not going to be sold some great distance from the sight of the theft, the rascals would go to work to change the appearance of the animal. Weight is the easiest to change. If the animal was thin they would feed it well; if it was overweight then they would reduce the intake. Hair dye was used to remove spots or add new ones. In the 1880s Mt. Vernon, Wisconsin, was experiencing a rash of horse thefts. After some time the thief was revealed to be the town's harness maker, C.J. Agrelius. Not to draw attention in Mt. Vernon, he would steal the area horses and take them to northwestern Illinois. Agrelius gains mention not because of his comparatively meager operation but due his method of disguise—of the horses. "One trick was to slice a potato, heat it and place it on the horse's forehead, thus branding off some of the hair. This changed the steed's black head to one with white on it, making the horse less recognizable to its owner. Agrelius was found guilty and sentenced to prison in Waupon. The 'Primrose Anti-Horse Thief Association,' was formed in 1891 as a result of Agrelius's crimes. After the formation of this association, no horse thefts were again committed."[4] Some rascals like Agrelius "have this art of changing the appearance of horses worked up to such perfection that a Kansas man who was suspicioned of having a hand in many stealing cases but never caught, once boasted that he could drive a horse thru the streets of the city in which it was stolen two days after the stealing and it would not be recognized."[5]

The single or solo horse thief was typically easier to catch than the gang operating with relay stations. The solo thief still needed a space to hide horses until the pursuit was over. Knowledge of the geography would always be of benefit in the search for horse thieves, who seemed to prefer "hilly and timbered" areas in which to hide out during the day before starting another night of travel away from the scene of the crime. Caves that were large enough could prove to be a great space for the solo or horse thief gang. In one account,

Graves related how one cave may have led a man to a higher calling of a horse thief.

In northern Kansas there was a minister who was noted for his strong oratory skills and frequently left to do missionary work and so he always had a couple of good horses about his farm. Located on a hill, the barn was built so it was partially underground. Locals knew that the minister was always in the habit of piling quite a bit of hay in one corner of the barn—unusual but chalked up to a harmless quirk. One day while the minister was gone, a man was "pitching manure" when he disturbed the pile of hay. A brief investigation showed that it covered a large door through which he heard a horse on the other side. Further investigation found six good horses in a cave in the hillside. It was assumed that the horses were turned out at night to get exercise and replaced in their hideout before dawn. After a period of time they would be taken elsewhere, always travelling at night. It could not be proven that the minister stole the horses— perhaps horse thieves hid them there from the unsuspecting minister. The Lord works in mysterious ways, as does the horse thief apparently.

"Barn Burners" were another type of despicable rascals. Uncovered by the Central Protection Association in Atchison, Kansas, this plan involved stealing a team of horses with little value and switching them with a good team then burning the barn down. The unsuspecting owner would find the burned remains of a team of horses and assume they were his, never realizing that his horses were being taken to another location to be sold. One gang did this in Atchison, burning two barns down, and another gang did likewise in Emporia, Kansas. In the Emporia case the farmer noticed that the burned horses had shoes while his horses were unshod. The Anti-Horse Thief Association captured the man but not until after two more barns were burned.

Scams played on liverymen were a common problem as well. In Chandler, Oklahoma, a man hired a team to drive to another town. Upon arrival he told this town's liveryman that his team was tired and he wanted to leave his team, switching for a fresh team to complete his journey. He also convinced the liveryman to loan him some money for he said was going to the next town to collect what was owed him then would return to pick up his team and pay off the loan. "We never learned just how many times he changed teams and how much money he borrowed but it is said he disappeared with the last team and has not been heard from since."[6]

Many horse thieves and other rascals would use an alias in their criminal activities. Many times this was to mask their actual identity to keep their families safe from retribution and knowledge of their criminal nature. The most common reason was that pseudonyms were part of the culture of the vanguard pioneers in the western expansion. A person's name meant much less than the bloodline of his horse. A man was judged by his work, knowledge of the range, and behavior. Names were not questioned and nicknames based on geography or physical attributes were common. "Flat Nose" Currie, Texas Pete, and "No Arm" Jack are just some examples. Some rascals would falsely use the name of a known, respectable person from a different part of the state to carry out their crimes. More than once a person of prominence would find that he was wanted for horse theft in a part of the state he had never visited. Identity theft is a crime that was well known to the horse thieves and rascals of the 1800s.

Order then Law

As horse thievery debased the safety and security currency people depended upon in their travels west, societies initially responded with two distinct methods: the mark and the pledge system. The mark system involved a common branding or mark of all member horses. A fee was paid to the association for each branded animal with a corresponding written record/description. This tradition

had been established since the 1700s, when horse owners
would be expected to record their designated "marks" with
the local government. The responsibility for these records
fell upon the anti-horse thief/ livestock societies during the
expansion era—often because towns would be settled before
any formal government was in place! The pledge system
required members of the various societies to respond when
members had a horse stolen. The inability to provide adequate law enforcement to the
expanding frontier was reluctantly recognized by states. As
independent anti-horse-thief societies started to spring up
across the country, state governments not only condoned
their creation, but often they would enhance their authority.

A Wisconsin law of 1861 authorized the "organization of
societies for mutual protection against larcenies of live
stock." The societies were given power to choose "riders" who
might "exercise all the powers of constables in the arrest and
detention of criminals." A similar law in Pennsylvania in 1869
incorporated the "Spring Valley Police Company of Crawford
County," a "company for the recovery of stolen horses and
other property." Its members were to have the same powers
of arrest and detention as policemen of Philadelphia.[7]

Volunteer policing, sanctioned by the government or not,
became an economic necessity in the frontier settlements.
In terms of volunteer policing, Martin Greenberg (2005)
refers to this era as the "vigilant era" characterized by "the
detective societies and posses (including slave patrols) of the
nineteenth century, as well as the rise of a score of antivice
societies." The names of many of these societies gave a clear
understanding to their purpose: Mount Hope Vigilant Society
for the Detection of Horse Thieves (New York, 1817); Society
in Roxbury, Brookline, and Brighton for Apprehending
Horse Thieves (Massachusetts, 1819); Anti Cattle and Horse
Thief Society of Freeborn County (Minnesota, 1862); and
Sheffield Association for the Detection of Horse Thieves

(Massachusetts, 1869). Other societies, who had as their mission the apprehension and return of stolen horses, had more innocuous names such as: Spring Valley Police Company of Crawford County (Pennsylvania, 1869); Cooper Vigilance Society (Michigan, 1879); and the Rising Sun Detective Association (Maryland, 1888).

As anti-horse-thief societies grew in stature and number, in New England they did not receive much support from state government. "State lawmakers may have tolerated the growth of protective societies in part because they were reluctant to tax all their citizens for extended police protection when crimes like horse stealing were prevalent only in certain well-defined areas."[8] In 1803 the Massachusetts House of Representatives created a committee that was to consider requiring several towns to form social compacts to pursue horse thieves. No action ever came as a result of this committee. That was not the case in New Jersey.

The state of New Jersey gave tacit approval of such societies until 1850, at which time it became a force of positive public policy. "An enactment of 1851 authorized the formation of associations for the protection of property. Ten or more citizens were permitted to meet within their township and establish a 'Protection Society, or Company.'"[9] The important feature of this act, and those that followed in the next ten years, was that it gave the power of arrest to members when they encountered anyone who had stolen property or were in possession of stolen property. In 1878 these powers were increased yet again.

In 1878, pursuers in New Jersey were invested with complete constabulary power. In 1884 the pursuers were required to file bonds with the county clerks in the amount of $5,000 should they engage in their work for members of the community at large; for the performance of their duties for society members, no bond was required. Yet another act passed in 1884 made it possible for the entire membership "upon view and without warrant, to apprehend and arrest all

persons committing breaches of the peace in any township
in which said society was organized."[10]

The Adoption of Anti-Horse Thief Association Laws

State	Year Authorized	Arrest Power Granted
New Jersey	1851	1878
Vermont	1851	
Indiana	1852	1852
New York	1859	1878
Michigan	1859	1859
Wisconsin	1861	
Kansas	1868	
Iowa	1870	
Missouri	1874	1874
Ohio	1885	1887
Nebraska	1885	1885
Illinois	1887	1887
Minnesota	1893	

Nolan 1987 in Greenberg 2005, 55

Many if not most of these societies had formal written
constitutions and by-laws. The Brush Valley Association
for the Detection and Apprehension of Horse Thieves was
formed on July 4, 1853 in Miles Township, Center County,
Pennsylvania. Their constitution states:

> We the undersigned citizens whose names are annexed
> believing in the importance of an associated effort for the
> prevention and arrestation of horse stealing and being
> desirous of forming a society to shield us from its evils and
> afford Mutual assistance in case of loss by theft, do herby
> agree to form ourselves into a society, for the purpose of
> concentrating our efforts on this object, and do herby adopt
> the following rules and regulations for our government.

If an animal was stolen, the president of the association

would "dispatch" eight or more members to give chase. Members were bound by association rules to continue their pursuit for up to fifty miles attempting to secure the stolen animal(s) and robber(s). Eight members would be sent out with the idea of two riding in each direction (North, South, East, and West). The riders were to keep track of any expenses incurred for reimbursement. If the horse was not recovered then the horse would be appraised and the "company" would be responsible for the payment to the member/victim.

The "riders" who were dispatched to pursue horse thieves were chosen for several reasons, including their ability to stop work and give chase at a moment's notice, the staying power of their personal mount, personal finances that would allow them to cover expenses while in pursuit (many of the time were property rich but cash poor), and personal knowledge, skill, and experience with similar responses. In some societies the positions of riders were elected or appointed by the president of the society. In some of the later and larger societies, the job or responsibility of rider fell upon every member. A typical story would be that which occurred in the fall of 1873 when Joe McClellan received notice that a gang of thieves had stolen horses from a neighbor just three hours before. "Joe, according to Mrs. J.B. Shields of Lost Springs, said, 'I will be ready in twenty minutes.' He ate a meager meal, took a small supply of food with him, and, after saddling his old faithful saddle-horse, Porter, and making sure of his Colt's revolvers, he was off. He was gone for about ten days."[11]

Sometimes horse thieves would try to take advantage of these operational practices. In July of 1874 a man giving the name Long from Sumner County rode into Fort Scott asking a Mr. Tannehill for a loan of money becuase he was in pursuit of a horse thief and had already depleted his meager resources. Knowing how the riders of the Anti-Horse Thief Association (A.H.T.A.) operate, this seemed in order and the amount was loaned to Long. Later, it was determined that

Long was in fact the horse thief and used this rouse to avoid suspicion. Tannehill and a local constable caught up with Long in Springfield, Missouri, in possession of three horses.[12]

If the riders were not successful then most of the societies would reimburse the owner through monies obtained as a "fine." Although the concept of reimbursement for horses not recovered was not common in New England, it became a selling point in the western societies. This led to an increase in motivation for the return of the horse for fiscal reasons as much as the satisfaction of a job well done. It was quickly noted by these societies that they had a vested interest in not just the detection and return of horses stolen, but in the prevention of theft. Prevention methods were approached through four main activities. The first method involved the swift and sure return of stolen horses and the capture of the guilty. The effectiveness and efficiency of the association would ensure it had more members, more resources, and better community support.

The second method was to publicize the existence of the society to serve as a warning to potential thieves. Broadsides and newspaper ads provided just as much prevention as notification to members. A potential horse thief would see the poster and know that although the area may be rich in horse flesh it also had an organized group of capable guardians who would send riders and spend money in their pursuit. The Kent (Connecticut) Society for Detecting Horse Thieves spent more than $160 in search of just one stolen horse in 1874.[13]

BOUND TO CATCH THE THIEF.
From the Detroit Free Press

Some of Miles Standish's old chums organized a horse thief detecting society in Rhode Island, the first society of the kind in the country. The ninety-fourth annual supper of the organization was recently given. The children and grandchildren of the original officers are running the society

Tulsa City-County Library
Central Library

Customer ID: **********1438

Items that you checked out

Title: Bullets, badges, and bridles : horse
thieves and the societies that pursued
them / by John K. Burchi
ID: 32345073653090
Due: **1/11/2020**

Title: Butch Cassidy : beyond the grave / W.C.
Jameson
ID: 32345049321517
Due: **1/11/2020**

Title: He rode with Butch and Sundance : the
story of Harvey "Kid Curry" Logan / by
Mark T. Smokov.
ID: 32345049444970
Due: **1/11/2020**

Title: Robbin' banks & killin' cops : the life and
crimes of Lawrence DeVol and his
association with Alvin
ID: 32345047387957
Due: **1/11/2020**

Total items: 4
Account balance: $0.00
2/28/2019 2:51 PM
Checked out 4

To renew:
www.tulsalibrary.org
18-549-7323

We value your feedback.
Please take our online survey.
www.tulsalibrary.org/Z45

to-day. In its career of ninety-four years it has lost but one horse, and for the detection of the thief who stole this animal two years ago over $2,000 has been expended. The hunt is still going on, as the old farmers who comprise the society would rather divide and squander all they have than admit that they were beaten.

—*New York Times,* November 11, 1890

The third method would be to ensure "justice" was done to those caught. Many anti-horse-thief societies made it clear that the members were to enforce the laws, return suspects to local law enforcement, and not take the law into their own hands. Some societies, if the horse was returned, would turn a blind eye to the disposition of those who took the animal.

The fourth method used was the encouragement of the use of bill of sale documents for a horse. Not unlike the title process of a modern car, a horse owner would be expected to prove to all potential buyers that he legally owned the horse. This practice is a vestige from England during the late sixteenth and early seventeenth centuries. "People interested in buying horses often insisted that sellers provide some proof or original ownership as protection against any later prosecution."[14] Persons filing indemnity petitions found little sympathy from juries or the courts when in possession of a stolen animal. Proof then, was in the papers. In a time when a man's word was as good as gold, a horse was worth more than a few words!

One of the problems of bringing law and order into the expanding western frontier was issues of jurisdiction. Crossing state lines may not have been a problem for the anti-horse-thief societies but it did pose problems for commissioned law enforcement officers. One remedy was the appointment of U.S. deputy marshals who could pursue horse thieves across state lines or into the territories. Fred Harrington gave the best description: "The deputies were simple men and expected danger as a part of each day's work."[15] A typical example was Captain Marks, a Native

American, and a U.S. deputy who worked for the "Hanging Judge" Parker. In 1881 Captain Marks held a warrant for Little Buck, an Osage horse thief who boasted that he would kill anyone who attempted to take him to Fort Smith for trial. This was proven out when Captain Mark's sworn in "posse" consisting of one E.M. Mathews was found dead, his body riddled with bullet holes.

Marks with his new "posse" did catch up with Little Buck, surrounded by his friends but unarmed. Marks called out in the Osage tongue that he had a warrant for Little Buck and asked if he would come in peacefully. Without his gun, Little Buck agreed. During an attempt to place the thief in handcuffs, Little Buck pulled a knife and Marks shot him in the leg. Although it was not his attempt to kill, Little Buck died that night. Knowing that Buck's friends were still out there, Marks was forced to "lay low" until he could safely return to Fort Smith. When he did return, he brought two additional horse thieves with him.[16]

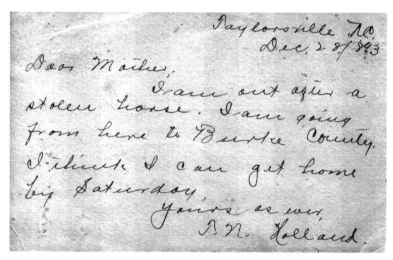

Dear Mother, I am out after a stolen horse. I am going from here to Burke County. I think I can get home by Saturday. Letter from J.N. Holland, December 28, 1893.

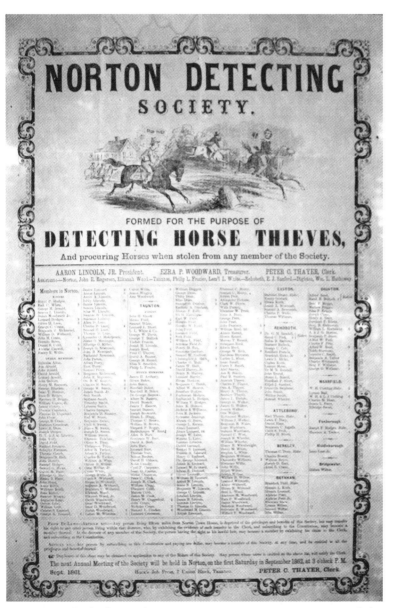

1861 Broadside from the Norton Detecting Society Formed for the Purpose of Detecting Horse Thieves and Recovering Horses, founded in 1791.

Sandlake Association for Mutual Protection Against Horse Thieves

Office of the Secretary
West Sandlake, N. Y.

FINE DUE

25

....Cents

Received Payment

Date *Nov. 18* 191*4*

Wm a. Ecker Secretary

RETURN THIS COMPLETE WITH FINE

If riders were not successful, most of the societies would reimburse the owner through monies obtained as a "fine."

Not all U.S. deputies stayed on the straight and narrow. Bob, Grat, and Emmett Dalton were officers working for Judge Parker who traded in their badge for the life of crime. The Daltons started their criminal career as horse thieves moving to train robbery and then bank robberies. They knew firsthand the difficulties faced in enforcement of the law in the frontier and had worked in supporting the law before they choose to change sides. It is interesting to note that their mother, Mrs. Louis Dalton, had the maiden name of Younger and her half brother was the father of the infamous Younger boys.[17]

Codes, Ciphers & Secret Societies

To make matters worse, organized horse thief gangs had a long history of communicating with other gangs and thieves, creating a loosely formed intelligence system that shared not just standard communication issues but the status of law enforcement investigations, where horses were being stolen and sold, which criminals were caught, offered assistance in escapes, and paid informants. "In August 1767 a Charleston newspaper described 'gangs of Villains' on 'the western frontiers' totaling two or three hundred men, who had 'for some years past infested those parts' and possessed 'regular communication with each other from the back settlements of Georgia to those of Virginia.'"[18] Within the limited law enforcement agencies of the time they "had spies and agents in their pay, 'Some to receive Goods and secret them-Others to give them Notice of Danger' . . . to take a wrong course in pursuit or to permit escape."[19] Many early anti-horse-thief associations formed because of poor communication with law enforcement—something already addressed by the thieves. When formed, and found to be successful, the anti-horse-thief associations gave the thieves a learning opportunity.

Not afraid to learn from those who pursued them, the horse thieves of the Black Hills formed a horse *thief* association. If the anti's could be so successful in the creation of formal societies that help detect horse theft, apprehend the offenders, and recover/return the stolen horses to their rightful owners, why not create a similar society for the commission of the crime of horse theft? "After capturing five outlaws in 1877, the army found the written 'constitution' of a large horsethief operation in the camp. Each member had been assigned a number in place of his name."[20] By the standards in place today, this would certainly be considered organized crime.

In Washington County, Nebraska, the people of the town De Soto created a "claim club" to protect the early settlers from having their land taken away by those who followed. This type of quasi-vigilante group was fairly common in the expansion era, but the people of De Soto never had an occasion to call the club up, and it soon died of natural causes. They would have been better served by creating an anti-horse-thief society, or at least some of them would have been better served. In late 1859 a young man was arrested on suspicion of being a member of a local band of horse thieves "which operated extensively in the vicinity, and was known to have its headquarters in or about the town." Upon the promise to be released, he informed his captors of the gang's location in a cave where there could be located "regularly drawn articles of organization, signed by the band." A review of the articles of organization and "other valuable documents" showed the names of many men, previously of high standing in the community, "and in consequence of their discovery, quite a number of De Soto's leading citizens immediately decamped, and the band of horse-thieves was effectually broken up, though not until several arrests had been made."[21]

During the daring raid across Indiana and Ohio in 1863, Confederate Gen. John Hunt Morgan "The King of Horse Thieves" brought with him the secret weapon of the South, "Lightning" George Ellsworth. A Canadian telegrapher working for the Confederacy, Ellsworth could tap into a telegraph line and after listening for a while could exactly mimic an operator's style. Each operator has a unique style or "fist" in operation of a telegraph key, allowing others to "know" that a message is legitimate. Being able deceive operators allowed Morgan to intercept messages and send out false orders, thus allowing them time to avoid their pursuers and continue their reign of destruction and horse theft.[22]

The December 4, 1902 edition of the *Anti Horse Thief Association Weekly News* has an article by Wm. B. Parker, first lieutenant of the Cedar Creek Lodge in Spurgeon, Missouri, of the South West Protective Association. In the article he calls for more cooperation between his organization and the Anti-Horse Thief Association. The article gives a peek into the covert side of anti-horse-thief society work. "Our written work you have, and our secret work is better for we know each other at sight and find members by night as well as day. Our able bodied men know the road. Our old men are placed on guard. In my judgment know we need to combine with all law and order associations and have a rogues' gallery of criminals and suspects so that when a man is missing we have a photo of him. If a suspect comes in, photograph him and pass it around and see where he is wanted."

The Central Protection Association, the South West Protective Association, the Anti-Horse Thief Association, and most other anti-horse-thief societies were secret organizations, in part, because of the intelligence reports collected and distributed of known and suspected criminals. Also secret were the signs and countersigns given between members, often at a distance, during pursuits. This was particularly important, as often riders in pursuit of horse thieves had to cross county and state jurisdictions to catch their prey.

Law enforcement had no method of sharing information between agencies that might lead to the arrest of suspects or the clearing of crimes, due to the distance between towns and poor communication systems. Horse thieves would use this chink in the armor of the law and steal horses in one area, sell them in another, and base their operation out of a third location. To apprehend these horse-thief gangs required work and information-sharing across several jurisdictions. One response was assigning deputy U.S. marshals who could cross jurisdictions. Another was the creation of the Rocky Mountain Detective Association. This association was a nongovernmental mutual-assistance league made up of various law enforcement agencies throughout the western frontier and northern Mexico.

The self reliance of the western frontier pioneer was also part and parcel of the western law enforcement officers' psyche. Lawmen tended to keep issues of enforcement in-house, calling on posses when needed, using only other lawmen or those who had served as lawmen. The idea of sharing information on unsolved crimes with other agencies was akin to admitting incompetence. The Rocky Mountain Detective Association changed that culture. Lawmen found that cases could be solved by sharing details, suspects located by sharing descriptions, and crimes averted by alerting other agencies of suspicious characters traveling through town. This agency did for all crimes what many anti-horse-thief associations were doing for the crime of horse theft.

Chapter 3

Societies Profiled

The idea that crime in general, and horse theft in particular, was never a problem until the late 1800s is wrong. It is true that the Old West frontier famously had problems with organized criminal gangs and horse thieves that congregated in bases with names such as "Robber's Roost" or "Hole in the Wall," but the colonies also had outlaw communities. In 1775 a gang of highwaymen created a fortified base in North Carolina from which to operate. The Higden band of horse thieves, which operated in South Carolina and Georgia, lived in a settlement on Rocky Comfort Creek, Georgia, "in open defiance of the whole country."[1]

"In 1769 a group of South Carolina frontiersmen chained John Harvey to a tree and took turns administering five hundred lashes while members of the party beat drums and played a fiddle. Harvey, a 'roguish and troublesome' man, was believed to have stolen a horse."[2] The "Regulators" had been hardened by several conflicts with Native Americans over land and with colonial officers imposing fees deemed illegal or excessive to these money-poor settlers. The "backwoodsmen" had fought and helped to clear the land, only to see a quasi-oligarchic handful of individuals begin to form a controlling government. Loss of their horse would be the economic death toll for these pioneers. They "had found it necessary to 'associate' in written agreements for the purpose of 'regulating' horse thieves by summary methods in the absence of efficient courts."[3]

The South Carolina Regulators stood up and called attention to the glaring contradictions of law and the authority that was not based in Charleston as claimed, but held its tenuous grip from "across the pond" in London. The actions taken by these men were with the best intention and for the long term interest of the area. "They believed in the rule of law. To that end they clamored for the introduction of a regular system of courts and sheriffs. By taking the law into their own hands the Regulators did defy the government. But they acted in the interest of true justice."[4]

The Back Country in 1759 had a population of about 20,000. Mostly white, they were ethnically diverse including groups of Germans, Swiss, Scotch-Irish, and Welsh. The Cherokee War (1760-61) resulted in a little more than a year of savage fighting, from both sides, that created a climate and culture of violence that morphed parts of the area into criminal havens, where violence was the norm. Many of "the outlaws, organized in vicious gangs, maintaining illicit ties with brigands and horse stealers in other colonies, and congregating in communities, presented a stern challenge to the Back Country. In 1766 these bandits launched a campaign of arson, torture, and robbery against the respectable element of the region."

The outlaws operated, originally, in groups no larger than twenty, but these gangs affiliated themselves into networks of gangs increasing the span of criminal control. The actions of the Regulators actually increased the resolve of the outlaws to coordinate their activities. A report from 1767 suggests that the "small parties" of outlaws created "places of general meeting, where (in imitation of councils of war) they form plans of operation and defense."[5]

The outlaws commonly formed themselves into organized gangs congregating in outlaw communities with their families, from wives and children to their parents. The women and children often helped in all aspects in support of the criminal actions of the community. These communities were not just safe havens but also became centers of learning the trade of horse theft and other crimes. "Elderly Persons, who have harbour'd Entertain'd, and Embolden'd these fellows, and taught them the Rudiments of ev'ry Vice."[6] As much as the very existence of these communities was offensive to the more respectable elements of South Carolina, it was their blatant campaign of arson and other crimes in 1766 that spurred the Regulators to respond because the government was not willing or able to carry out the law. No one was immune to the actions of these gangs. In 1767, Gov. William Tryon of North Carolina lost several horses after an encounter with a gang.

Throughout outlaw history, they continued to use these fortified centers for outlaw gangs established by these communities, such as their "rabbit holes" and "hideouts." For horse thieves a hideout had to include space to stable horses. In 1793 Connecticut, "Just over the Woodstock line in the town of Ashford, desperados had sought out the summit of a high hill, thickly wooded and covered with a dense growth of underbrush, and built a stockade or horse pound in which they would put stolen horses until such time as they would dispose of them safely, and it was a long time before the rendezvous of the gang was discovered and broken up."[7]

The law is one method used to regulate social behavior, with agents of the government acting as the enforcers. By 1767 it was clear that the law and its enforcement agents were only effective for the control of law abiding citizens. "Driven by desperation by the inroads of the outlaws and unprotected by the provincial court, respectable Back Countrymen 'rose in a Body' and assaulted 'the Villains-burning of their Cabbins and Camps—taking away the Goods and Horses, and Young Girls they had carried off."[8] Not supported by the government, the actions quickly transformed the mob into the "Regulators" who pledged to bring order to the Back Country and to support one another.

The government's passive response to the Regulator movement was a clear indication of awareness that the

complaints of injustices and inability to bring order was not
without merit. The Regulators held court, and punishment
ranged from banishment to hanging. Often horse thieves
were whipped or burned on the hand. As settlements began
to grow, and the backwoods were no longer being considered
the frontier, the people petitioned for annexation and formal
law. When law and order became common, the need for the
Regulators faded. Soon the country began to feel a little too
crowded and the expansion west began, bringing with it many
of the ghosts of the South Carolina Back Country. A new
breed of Regulators began to emerge to act as exorcists—the
anti-horse-thief societies.

The Central Protection Association
With the Civil War well under way, raiders and outlaws like
the James brothers were engaged in so much criminal activity
that farmers in Clay County, Missouri felt that their lives let
alone their horses were no longer safe. In 1863, a Missouri
farmer had it tough, trying to keep crops and livestock
thriving and protected not just from the hazards of weather
and chance, but from outlaws. "The farmer who owned an
extra good pair of horses did not know at what hour in the day
or night they would disappear." Reaching a breaking point,
twenty-five area farmers gathered together and "every horse
thief they caught they hanged to a tree. Acting spontaneously
they took matters in their own hands, as they thought they
were obliged to do so for their own protection."⁹
Realizing that "the time came when the men must suit
their actions to the law, lest some innocent man be a
victim," the Central Protective Association was formed in
1870. Birthed from a clearly vigilante group, they took great
pains to disavow similar actions from their members. Like
so many of the anti-horse-thief societies of the time, they
had little faith in the effectiveness of local law enforcement.
"With little to fear from police or sheriffs, there would be
nothing to hinder these criminals making raiding tours were

it not for the protection which is given by the volunteer organization of farmers and citizens that is known as the Central Protection Association." Membership was open to any "well recommended white man" of eighteen years of age or older, and women were allowed to join for the protection of stock, but they did not have the same rights as their male counterparts. Widows of members had privileges:

> The widow of a deceased brother, who was in good standing at the time of his death, shall be entitled to all benefits of the Association during her widowhood by the payment of the dues and assessments required by By-Laws and it shall be the duty of the Secretary to notify her of her rights immediately upon the death of her husband. Any white widow may become an honorary member.[10]

Although created to fight horse theft, the Central Protection Association (CPA) followed the lead of other anti-horse-thief societies and expanded their scope to other crimes as well. One type of organized crime was known as "riding the circle." One large or main gang would disperse its members into small groups who would travel along preset routes, roughly a large oval or circle, in a covered wagon. Routes in this case had Omaha at one end and Kansas City at the other. Stealing anything deemed of value along the way, they would create caches of stolen property along the route and if approached by law enforcement they would feign innocence and allow their wagons to be searched. When they passed other members going the opposite direction, they would tell them the location of the cache of stolen items. The CPA in one of its annual meetings, gathered reports from the lodges and was able to piece together the operation. "Had not a strong organization of determined men taken up the work of their capture it is probable that it would have been many months or perhaps years before the gang was broken up."[11]

The CPA had accumulated enough members and resources that some local lodges owned the buildings in which they met. In 1903 the president of the CPA, W.S. Connor (a legislator in the Missouri House) reported that Atchison County, Kansas, had 800 members with 22 subordinate lodges. The CPA formed a partnership with the Anti-Horse Thief Association, which included sending delegates to the national convention of each association and a monthly "Page of the Central Protective Assoc't'n The Allies of the A.H.T.A." in the *Anti-Horse Thief Weekly News*.

In 1917 there were more than three hundred branches of the CPA located in Kansas, Nebraska, and Missouri with membership in the thousands. Although formed primarily for horse theft, the CPA covered other crimes as well. The Wathena chapter (Doniphan County, Kansas) CPA No. 18 in 1917 had more than 350 members and had a standing reward for burglary in the amount of $50.00 and a $100.00 reward for the capture of a horse thief.

The *coup de grace* for the CPA, like so many other anti-horse-theft societies, was the creation of state police, more efficient local police and telecommunications, and the automobile. Most chapters of the CPA soon became forgotten history but not in Eudora, Kansas. Near the town center, Eudora has the CPA Park. Each year they hold a CPA picnic and more recently the Horsethief 5 K race. The picnic has been a tradition since 1901 although 1946 saw the picnic cancelled "at the request of County and State Health Authorities who are alarmed over the spread of infantile paralysis or polio."[12]

Consolidated Vigilant Society of
New Jersey and Pennsylvania

Formed in 1891, the Consolidated Vigilant Society of New Jersey and Pennsylvania was one of the first of the multi-state anti-horse-theft societies. The full title was the Consolidated Vigilant Society of New Jersey and Pennsylvania for the Recovery of Stolen Horses and Other Property, and the Detection of Thieves. Individual societies could apply to

join and would be required to send delegates to the annual meeting. "With such others as may associate with us for the purpose of promoting the interest and increasing the usefulness of each individual society, do hereby agree to unite our several societies into one society, for the uses and purposes hereinafter named."[13] Benefits included the sharing of reported thefts and pursuers who could cross state lines with much greater ease than the local and state law enforcement officers.

The Farmers' Alliance

Many of the anti-horse-thief societies were the largest and most influential fraternal organizations of the community. Businessmen and community leaders would join more for the political power gained through association with the organization, than concern over stolen stock. Because the meetings were secret, this could allow for subtle business deals and political alliances to be made. One anti-horse-thief society that started in Texas, the Farmers' Alliance, eventually became the Populist Party.

Originally organized in Lampasas County, Texas in 1874 or 1875, the alliance was the outcropping of the frustration of area farmers with the gangs of horse thieves, cattle rustling, and feuds that were becoming so common. Because all of the founding members were farmers, not much imagination was required for the name. It was a secret fraternal organization in every sense and grew quickly, "like wild fire in Texas and the South in the 1880's [sic]."[14] The tough economic conditions and the rise of the "Fence-Cutters War" added fuel to this wild fire. Within twenty years this organization had grown from local to regional to national. "Conditions of economic hardship for the farmers of central Texas in the 1880s transformed the quasi-vigilante Farmers' Alliance into a nonviolent political and economic movement for broad agrarian reform."[15]

The evolution of the Farmers' Alliance from anti-horse-thief society to the Populist Party did not go unnoticed among other similar societies. Although most societies would state in their constitutions or bylaws that they were not political organizations, they often engaged in political activities that would benefit, at the very least, the overall aims of their organization. From legislation authorizing the power of arrest for their members to maintaining rail lines, many anti-horse-thief societies watched and learned from this Texas organization.

Independent Order of the Knights of the Horse
Formed in 1884 by Charles Dennis with G.B. Scott as grand president, the Independent Order of the Knights of the Horse was an anti-horse-thief society organized with lodges in Arkansas. Very little primary source documentation could be located on this organization but they did merge with the national fraternal organization, the Anti-Horse Thief Association, in 1902. An account of the merger was reported in the *Anti-Horse Thief Weekly News* on August 14, 1902. It stated:

National President Scott, Editor Graves, and President Corbin
of the Missouri division spent a couple of days near Siloam
Springs last week...They attended the Independent Order of
the Knights of the Horse, an order almost identical with the
A.H.T.A. and working along the same object in view. This
order has been doing good work in Arkansas since the early
seventies, but covered no outside territory. It was composed
of active and earnest men, anxious to promote their common
interests....received several letters from President Scott
concerning the A.H.T.A. and were very favorably impressed...
Only two delegates in the convention opposed the move
and when the vote to consolidate was taken, it was almost
unanimous. Two A.H.T.A. sub-orders were organized during
the afternoon in the same room in which the I.O.K.H. held its
meeting and another was organized at a school house a few
miles distant the same evening....Horses stolen in Arkansas
were taken to the territory or some other point out of range
of the I.O.K.H. the consolidation of the two orders will in time
put an end to this practice and be of benefit to all parties
concerned except the thieves.

National Horse Thief Detective Association
The National Horse Thief Association is the repackaged and
enhanced manifestation of the Wabash General Association
of Detective Companies (see below). Their primary activities
were focused on the coordination and education of the many
anti-horse-thief societies located in the state of Indiana.
An attempt to expand the operations beyond the borders
of Indiana was met with limited success, with member
chapters found in Ohio and Illinois. Many of the chapters
counted influential members of the local community among
their ranks, which helped with recruitment and support of
local anti-horse-thief societies. In 1898 the president of the
National Horse Thief Detective Association was James A.
Mount, governor of Indiana.
    The state of Indiana gave members the powers of arrest,
which was effectively used in the detection and apprehension

of horse thieves. As the number of horse thefts declined, many members turned their powers of arrest to other crimes such as intoxication, and public support of the group started to wane. Some local newspapers made it a crusade to cover what was deemed the exercise of extralegal authority. Membership started to decline and by "the twentieth century the N.H.T.D.A. was little more than a social organization, and by 1930 only a few scattered companies held an occasional meeting."[16] It was the alliance of the National Horse Thief Detective Association with the Ku Klux Klan that led the state legislature to rescinded the power of arrest to any secret society, including anti-horse-thief detective societies, on March 9, 1933. The passage of this legislation "proved a death blow to the national organization"[17] although it took many years before the national and local units dissolved.

Newton Reliance Company for Detecting and Apprehending Horse Thieves and Other Villains

Many anti-horse-thief societies started as a purely voluntary organization formed to meet the specific need of protecting livestock. With a clear and common purpose in mind, this Pennsylvania fellowship banded together without dispute and proved to be effective in their cause. The Newton Reliance Company operated from 1819 through 1865 before they applied for legal status as a formal, incorporated entity. Once they organized formally disputes arose, and in 1867 two new anti-horse theft societies were formed. The exact nature of the split may have been in dispute but the structure and success of the Newton Reliance Company was not and it proved so effective that it soon became an example for the creation of many other societies in surrounding communities.

The Newton Reliance Company established preset routes for pursuers to follow when called upon. These routes were a carefully guarded secret of the society and covered all known routes that thieves could consider. The company remained active throughout the years and in 1914 voted to include automobiles under their umbrella of protection. Still in existence today, this society continues to appoint the appropriate positions but acts more as a social and community civic group.

Southwest Missouri Protective Association

Very much akin to the CPA, the Southwest Missouri Protective Association was formed to provide similar work in a part of the state not covered by the CPA. It was formed in 1886 due to the large amount of horse theft that was occurring in Jasper, McDonald, and Newton counties. The problem continued to grow until forty head of horses were stolen in a ten-mile strip of Jasper County. In February 1886, Wm. B. Parker and John Thrasher went to Jasper County and organized the protective association. They met at the Prairie Flow school house located two miles west of Webb City, the general location of the theft of the forty head of horses. "The Southwest Missouri Protective Association is an order of a few hundred members and some fifteen local lodges located near Joplin, Neosho, Carl Junction and other points in Missouri. It's [sic] workings are very much like the A.H.T.A. and C.P.A. and it has about the same purpose in view."[18] Lacking a strong central organizing ability, the Southwest Missouri Protective Association allied itself with the CPA and the AHTA.

Union Horse Company

A "Horse Company" was a term often used for anti-horse-thief societies as was the case in Doylestown Township, Pennsylvania. On November 18, 1834 the following notice appeared in the local paper:

The citizens of Doylestown township and its vicinity are invited to attend a Meeting to be held at the house of JACOB FREESE, Turk's Head, on Saturday, the 6th of December, to take into consideration the propriety of forming a Horse Company.[19]

The meeting resulted in the creation of the Union Horse Company of Doylestown Township and its Vicinity for the Detecting and Apprehending of Horse Thieves and Other Villains. The original members read like a who's who of the local community with many prominent businessmen on the rolls. All members were subject to being called out in pursuit of stolen horses following preset routes, which could be exceeded should the pursuit team believe that they are on the route used by the thief. The routes were considered secret and there would always be two persons assigned to a route. The routes were numbered with directions and the president would write the names of the pursuers on these slips and pass them out when the company was called out. Many of these route slips have been preserved and the following are two examples:

No. 23—To the County0 Line, Hatborough, Foxchase, Philadelphia by second street road, and return by Germantown.
No. 24—To the Buck Tavern, Bustleton, Cornwell's Tavern, Holmsburg, Point Road to Philadelphia, and back at discretion.[20]

More than thirty routes were created to cover all the possible exit points that a thief might take. Horseback and carriage were the only modes of transportation, other than by foot. Records show that there were several modifications made to the routes through the years, but there were no records kept as to the number of thefts and the success or failure of the pursuits. The route system of deployment was eventually abandoned in 1891 and replaced by a detective system, in which ten members would be assigned the task of tracking and apprehending the horse thieves.

The Union Horse Company became a member of the Grand Consolidated Vigilant Society of New Jersey and Pennsylvania in 1946 and continues to meet, more than 170 years since its creation, as a social organization.

Wabash General Association of Detective Companies

Formed in 1860 the Wabash General Association of Horse Thief Detective Companies was created as an effort to consolidate the various societies within the state of Indiana. The organizational structure was similar to most of the anti-horse-thief societies, although they appear to be the first to encourage members from similar organizations to sit in their meetings. In the president's address to the members on August 10, 1880, President John Gray stated, "For twenty years our body has stood as a terror to evil-doers, and through our instrumentality and unite efforts much property has been restored to rightful owners, and perpetrators of crime have been made to atone to the offended law. . . . The marauders who infest our land, and the thieves and vagabonds who prowl through the country appropriating that which does not belong to them, have been made to feel that we dare to do right and to protect and defend the property which belongs to us and to our neighbors."[21]

The individual lodges were recorded by number but came with no common name although many incorporated "detectives" into their individual chapter name. Examples include: Liberty Police Rangers; Wesley Association; Shawnee Mound Minute Men; Newell Horse Co.; Iroquois Union Guards; Walnut Grove Detectives; Dry Run Detectives; Lawrence Horse Thief Company; and the Centennial Horse Thief Detective Company. Like so many similar organizations, the primary focus of origin was horse theft but quickly morphed into including the detection and apprehension of other felonies.

The distinctive feature of the societies profiled in this chapter was their specific purpose to turn the horse thieves over to the proper authorities. Even if they started more as vigilant groups, they quickly morphed into societies who did their best to follow the law. As the country continued its westward journey, it was the vigilante committees that would most likely blaze the trail for the detection, apprehension, and administration of justice.

Chapter 4

Vigilante

. . . It becomes an absolute necessity that good, law-loving, and order sustaining men should unite for mutual protection, and for the salvation of the community. Being united they must act in harmony; repress disorder; punish crime, and prevent outrage, or their organization would be a failure from the start, and society would collapse in the throes of anarchy. None but extreme penalties inflicted with promptitude, are of any avail to quell the spirit of the desperadoes with whom they have to contend; considerable numbers are required to cope successfully with the gangs of murderers, desperadoes and robbers, who infest mining countries and who, though faithful to no other bond, yet all league willingly against the law. Secret they must be, in council and membership, or they will remain nearly useless for the detection of crime, in a country where equal facilities for the transmission of intelligence are at the command of the criminal and the judiciary; and an organization on this footing is a Vigilance Committee.[1]

Horses and their theft were directly related to the lawlessness of the western frontier. Since the colonial era the horse has often been the vehicle used, if not the item taken, in the commission of a crime. Horse thieves "acted as parasitic growths upon frontier life retarding forces to the development of the country," creating a contagion phenomenon for other crime until the people had enough.[2] Conflict is a universal cultural concept and in the United States there is a strong tradition of "repeated episodes of violence, going far back into our colonial past, [which] have imprinted upon our citizenry a propensity to violence. Our history has produced and reinforced a strain of violence, which has strongly tinctured our national experience."[3] When the solution to conflict is unrestrained violence outside of any established legal institution, then society enters the dark and bitter realm of vigilantism.

Vigilantism is the communal desire and action of private citizens, or of government agents acting outside of their official capacity, to enforce existing law or to reestablish social norms of the community. The action may also be an attempt to end a cycle of behavior deemed deviant as viewed through a criminal, cultural, or political lens. Vigilantism breaks "existing law to serve the future for the law."[4]

In the West and Midwest, committees and societies were formed to protect property scarce resources, and to combat ineffective law enforcement during times of expansion. Many times these organizations were created specifically to fight horse thieves. When the fight involved extralegal violence, by good or bad men in the name of any organization, for any purpose including horse theft, this becomes known as vigilantism.

This country was founded on the principle of freedom. Freedom built upon the "American notion of popular sovereignty, self-preservation, and the right to revolution, a belief inherited from the American Revolution that government was ultimately rooted in the people and could, if threatening circumstances dictated, be reclaimed by them."[5] Law enforcement agencies operate in a continuum that ranges from one side, where law enforcement tells the community what the enforcement priorities are and how they will address them, to the other end where the community tells law enforcement what it has identified as the priorities and is asking law enforcement to help it address the issues. This was true 150 years ago and is true today. When law enforcement operates on one end of the continuum and the community on the other, role strain and conflict are inevitable.

Identified Names of Vigilante Groups

Citizen's Committee	Committee of Safety	Committee of Vigilance
Detective Associations	Mobs	Protective Associations
Rangers	Regulators	Slickers
Stranglers	White Caps	

Often vigilante groups were created out of frustration because of the incompetence, inability, or outright refusal of the government to take action. "In eastern Iowa between April and December 1857, landed vigilantes had collectively murdered sixteen white men whom they accused of horse theft, counterfeiting, and murder."[6] There seemed to be a cultural lag of law and order on the frontier that shaped the character of the early settler. Texas of 1888 was a country where the public took little concern over an "ordinary killing." If at trial the suspect could make a case of self defense there was a very good chance of acquittal. "But horse stealing was another matter, something to be taken seriously." The response was simple: "hang 'em first any time you could catch them."[7] This was not a uniquely Texas response to dealing with disorder. Throughout the western plains and mountains "frontiersmen viewed the horse thief as worse than a murderer. The cattleman had to use horses in his daily work. Without them he was almost helpless. Unhorsed far from home, he was exposed to every danger in the wilds."[8] This meant that those who stole horses could expect no mercy, and in cases of organized horse thief gangs, frequent and spontaneous vigilante committees could be expected. "Any good calf rope could be used in decorating a tree."[9]

Popular Sovereignty

One of the underlying causes of vigilante action towards horse thieves, or any citizen deemed guilty of deviant behavior, is the concept of popular sovereignty. People began to rely much more frequently on their ability to organize in all forms of extralegal groups and societies, as they first experienced in the American Revolution. Richard Maxwell Brown[10] lists forty colonial riots occurring from 1641 through 1759 creating a heritage of resistance in the American psyche. "In 1787 Samuel Chase of Maryland declared that the people's power 'is like the light of the sun, native, original, inherent, and unlimited by human authority. Power in the rulers or governors of the people is like the reflected light of the moon and is only borrowed, delegated and limited by the grant of the people.'"[11] There is a historical connection between this concept and the authority used to create many of the vigilante groups and anti-horse-thief societies.

Common was the theme that when the established government was impotent or blind to the crime and moral decay of a community, the people were endued with the authority and right to rise up and reestablish order. One example was the bandit and "blackleg" criminal communities of Noble County in northern Indiana. Founded in the early 1830s, these criminal communities supported and protected each other as they carried out horse theft, murder, arson, and counterfeiting. This went on for some twenty-five years ending in 1858 when 2,000 regulators rose and ended the reign of crime. The regulators clearly stated their beliefs in the first of their resolutions in January 1858:

> Whereas, We are believers in the *doctrine of popular sovereignty;* that the people of this country are the real sovereigns, and that whenever the laws, made by those to whom they have delegated their authority, are found inadequate to their protection, it is the right of the people to take the protection of their property into their own hands, and deal with these villains according to their just desserts . . .[12]

Like a tsunami surging across the plains, the doctrine of popular sovereignty moved westward leaving the destructive effects of vigilantism in its wake. "Popular sovereignty was attractive to settlers not only because it gave them the authority to act in their own best interests but also because it was consistent with natural law's edict that each person had the right and the responsibility to protect his own life and property in the absence of other protection."[13] Despite the initial outrage/debate at the use of popular sovereignty in the resolution of the crimes in Noble County, Indiana, anti-horse-thief societies used the same justification in their charters.

Protection of personal property, be it a home or a horse, seemed to have widespread support and when vigilante action was used to stop others from taking the property, it was often met with tacit approval. The general support changed when the concept of property and the doctrine of popular sovereignty were applied to slavery. "While debating Senator Stephen Douglas in the fall of 1858, Abraham Lincoln declared the principle of popular sovereignty, as applied to the Kansas Territory, to be 'nothing but a living, creeping lie from the time of its introduction till today.'"[14] Douglas used the concept of popular sovereignty as a campaign slogan and a driving force in the legislation of the creation of the Kansas and Nebraska Territories. It was a concept that acted as a catalyst on both sides of the dark days of "bloody Kansas." It was debated in most households and communities and stayed a common yet pejorative topic through the western expansion and the Civil War. Strongly tied to the concept of slavery, the principle of popular sovereignty did find a broader base of support among the frontier townsfolk who often endured crime with little to no government support. For this group the principle of popular sovereignty became the base of the frontier theory of vigilantism.

Frontier Theory of Vigilantism
The frontier, be it the Allegheny Mountains, the Mississippi

River, the Rocky Mountains, or the West Coast, seems to have been the backdrop for the rise and fall of vigilante groups. "Frontiers pose particular problems for the administration of criminal justice. For example, as a general rule, issues of deviance and social control are magnified on geographical frontiers."[15] In this theory, the lack of adequate law enforcement during this strain between deviance and social control would leave "crime-besieged citizens with no alternative but to take the law into their hands."[16] This theory does not state that all frontiers were or will be in a state of anarchy. There are many cases of frontier areas settled with little violence or crime. The frontier theory of vigilantism suggests that when crime occurs unchecked by the government or citizens, it acts like a contagion creating more crime and fear until the citizens decide that it is time to amputate. We should remember that "at no other time in the history of the world were there so many spoils to be divided among the swift, the strong, and the oppressed: land, game, furs, minerals, timber, grass, and water. Everything considered, it is miraculous that the last and largest frontier region in the United States was settled in as orderly a fashion as it was."[17]

Although the primary focus of this work is on criminal deviance, the frontier theory would also attempt to explain the creation of vigilante groups that formed various committees to deal with the social ills of the time. The South Carolina Regulators in the mid 1700s often focused on moral regulation. In Woodbury, New Jersey, in 1809 the Whirligig Society was created to "suppress all riots, and Whirligig all Gamblers, Showmen and such characters as are commonly styled fair plays; that happen to intrude upon the peaceable, moral and respectable inhabitants." Another early example from New Jersey (1827) was the Readington, Tewksbury, and Lebanon Society for the Suppression of Vice and Immorality, and for the Promotion of Virtue and Good Morals.[18] The frontier theory would also explain the

White Cap movement that first appeared in Indiana in 1887 and spread throughout the country. "White capping was most prevalent as a sort of spontaneous movement for the moral regulation of the poor white and ne'er-do-wells of the rural American countryside."[19] They also included abusive spouses and "loose women" in their punishments that ranged from public humiliation and whippings to banishment.

The frontier theory suggests that there would be similar actions in other frontier regions, such as the peasant justice against horse thieves in Russia of the 1800s where "frontier areas attracted horse thieves because of the distance from the central administration and its more effective policing powers."[20] Villages created teams of people to carry out extralegal actions. In one horse-theft case the people of the village concluded, "'Let us punish him better ourselves . . . so that his legs will walk less around the yards belonging to others.' The peasants placed their victim face down on the ground, applied pressure to his knees, and struck his heels a few times with a log, crippling the man for life." The frontier theory also can be applied to the modern inner city, where thieves are attracted to the lack of effective policing and the "crime-besieged citizens" take the law into their own hands attacking crack houses and gang hideouts. Impatient or dissatisfied with the government, its agents, and its courts, 1800s vigilantism rises with the same resolve as their pioneer forefathers, according to frontier theory.

Knowing that their actions were illegal, people developed a philosophy of vigilantism to legitimize the actions of vigilantes. This philosophy included self-preservation, the right of revolution, and popular sovereignty.[21] The concept of popular sovereignty grew quickly to become the primary stated reason for vigilantism in the nineteenth-century western expansion. To settle the frontier required different social norms than that of the established communities. The country was changing fast, and the people did not like to consider the law as a social restraining device safeguarding against the whims of change.[22] When the courts began to become established in the frontier, they faced this fact with some difficulty.

Order in the Court

Not all courts were created equal. Some courts had little supervision and some were community courts not recognized by the state. Maj. Horace Bell recalled his exposure to the early "court" in the City of Angels. He described the building as a small, two-room adobe house "in which sat in solemn conclave, a sub-committee of the great constituted criminal court of the city." He found that they had been in session for a week trying to "extract confessions" from the six men being held. "Finally one Reyes Feliz made a confession, probably under the hypothesis that hanging would be preferable to such inquisitorial torture as was being practiced by on him by the seven wise men of the Angels." In his confession he stated that he and his brother-in-law, Joaquin Murietta, and a few others had stolen horses belonging to Jim Thompson. They made it as far as the Tejon when Zapatero, the Tejon chief, recognized the brand as belonging to Jim Thompson and arrested them. Once captured he stripped them all naked, "tied them up, and had them whipped half to death, and turned them loose to shift for themselves in the best way that they could." The chief returned the horses to Thompson and the guilty eventually made their way to Los Angeles.[23]

Armed with the confession and the intent to carry out "justice," this early "court" had the unintended consequence to birth one of the most notable outlaws of the southwest. "At the time this confession was made, Joaquin was walking around, as unconcerned as any other gentleman; but when the minions of the mob went to lay heavy hand upon him he was gone, and from that day until the day of his death, Joaquin Murietta was an outlaw and the terror of the southern counties."

Sentencing practices were also unique. The report of the

findings of the committee on Reyes Feliz was read aloud by the president of the committee who then said:

"'Gentlemen, the court is now ready to hear any motion.' Whereupon a ferocious looking gambler mounted a bench and said:
'I move that Reyes Feliz be taken to the hill and hung by the neck until he be dead.'
'All in favor of the motion will signify the same by saying aye!' said the President, gravely.'
'Aye! aye! aye!' yelled the mob, and Reyes Feliz was a doomed man."[24]

In another case in the same session of the court involving murder, not horse theft, the motion was made to turn the man "over to the constituted authorities," which passed without any dissenting vote.

On February 26, 1851 in Sacramento City a fight broke out between a gambler and a miner. The gambler and a companion were beating the miner so severely (the man did die of the beating, leaving behind a wife and five children) that a citizen stepped up and attempted to part them, stating that if they were to fight, fight fair—not two against one. The gambler shot this man in the head, killing him instantly. It was at this time that the wheels of justice started to turn, and they turned at great speed. "In eight hours time [after] the man [was] shot, the prisoner [was] arrested, and the jury appointed, the prisoner [was] tried and strung up by the neck; and this is California speed in bringing culprits to Justice."[25]

To create law and order in the expanding west, federal courts were established in territories. Many of the judges assigned to these courts were "considered to be carpetbaggers receiving relatively undesirable appointments for political services rendered in the East. Their continuous quarrels with [other] unpopular judges led to forced resignations or 'sagebrushing'—assignment to a district where judicial business was almost nonexistent or where riding circuit was too difficult." This situation created open hostility between the citizens and the court. On top of the dubious appointments, "the administration of justice was neither swift nor of the highest quality."[26] Sometimes this displeasure was even shown by frontier decorum in the courtroom. In a court case held at Fort Griffin in 1877, a judgment was rendered against John B. Carn. Mr. Carn demonstrated his displeasure by knocking out the judge, the clerk, and opposing counsel. He then left the courtroom where no contempt of court charges were levied. Decorum was also showcased by lawyer J.L. Adams who, in 1889, was being charged for using "boisterous language" in Mason, Texas. When the county attorney made an objection to the introduction of a witness, Adams picked up a chair and attempted to break it over the head of the prosecutor. Quick on his feet, the county attorney deflected the blow and only broke a finger. Adams' actions so pleased the jury that they promptly acquitted him.[27]

In many cases the judge had a circuit to travel and would hold court in any available public building, often the local saloon. "Motions put by dry spectators, to adjourn for a wet refresher, always carried." And "in Oklahoma, the official crier at the federal court used to open the proceedings by shouting, 'Hear ye! Hear ye! Now all you mully-grubs in the back of the courtroom keep your traps shut and give these swell guys up in front a chance to talk!'" Fines ordered by the court also posed unique problems because many had little cash. One defendant who was found guilty of contempt was fined a blanket for the judge and "a pair of breeches for the United States Marshall."[28]

Getting a defendant to court could prove a logistical nightmare. The early court system in Texas, for example, typically would be placed in the county seat but that meant that it could be a journey of a hundred miles or more for the ranchers. "The outpost of justice was too remote to take all cases there. Men often took law into their own hands and were judge, jury, and at times, executioner. But the Cattlemen of the Panhandle did not want to mete out justice; they wanted only protection while they put flesh on cows and took them to market."[29] If the government could not provide what was needed, the self-reliant settlers would.

The attempts to provide civil authority in the territorial west proved difficult and often ended with resentment when it was put into play. This legal lag could not effectively deal with horse thieves and cattle rustlers, so the people rose up, creating organizations that acted as popular courts. The freedom from crime and the fear of crime has been the holy grail that societies have searched for since Jamestown. The dream of the quest's end, where all are bathed in the warm glow of justice, meant that the knights (or in this case settlers) could answer a higher law, slaying the dragon with lethal violence if the formal legal system would not. For some, this was nothing more than an act of chivalry on behalf of the community; other knights would sleep the restless sleep of the warrior, forever reminded of battles fought. Order had to be brought to the realm and it was not happening in a swift and sure manner in the territorial west.

The dichotomy of this Arthurian saga played out time and time again in the Old West. As the courts and law enforcement proved ineffective, the people created organizations and societies under a variety of names from Anti-Horse Thief Associations to Committees of Vigilance, all with the express purpose of bringing order to the community, something the early criminal justice agencies could not or would not do. The people of Aurora, Nevada, in 1864 had reached their breaking point and a group called the "Protective Union" gathered all the nefarious characters and yet-to-be-convicted criminals and banished them from town. The Protective Union with the help of the local militia also hung four persons. Tucson, Arizona, saw the murder of a business man and his wife in the 1870s and the people of

Tucson, outraged with the murder and the slow and sporadic effectiveness of the courts, created a safety committee who tracked down the three guilty parties and to effect swift and sure punishment issued the following statement:

> You have been proved guilty of this crime, and you must all prepare to die tomorrow. You need not hope to escape through legal trickery of court delay; there will be no further trial. The people of Tucson have found you guilty, and the citizens themselves will hang you.[30]

In Texas, the number of lynchings for horse theft started to decline in the 1880s when more were willing to let the court system handle the sentences. "The courts seemed to be able to handle horse stealing cases with more dispatch than any other type of case. . . . trials were swift, conviction sure, and sentences heavy."[31] Texas also saw the most effective law enforcement agency for the capturing of horse thieves: the Texas Rangers. They quickly obtained the rightful reputation of trailing, capturing, and returning horse thieves to the courts in which they were wanted.

Badges and Brigands

In the 1860s Idaho had an influx of horse thieves and "desperados" who seemed to thrive regardless of any complaints made to territorial authorities. The response was the creation of vigilante committees. One committee, the Payette vigilance committee, used several methods of punishment: banishment, horsewhipping, and death. "It cleared the Payette Valley of horse thieves in three months." These Idaho "committees" had a little more difficult task in the spring of 1866 with their attempt to stop a band of horse thieves and outlaws led by David Updyke, the corrupt sheriff of Ada County. On April 3, a young man who had testified against the gang was murdered by one of its members. Custody in Fort Boise did not offer enough protection for the young witness as he was taken from the guardhouse by

Boise vigilantes and hung. Updyke and another member of his gang fled but were also found hung, badge and all.[32] In 1864 Aurora, Nevada, the people had had enough after losing thirty of their citizens to violence in just three years. The murder of a man who refused to tell a gang who had killed one of the gang members for horse theft proved to be the breaking point. The good people of Aurora formed a "Citizens' Protective Union" and started a roundup of the local outlaws. Three ring leaders were caught and jailed. Members of the protective union started construction of a scaffold, which caused someone to notify the governor in Carson City. The governor sent a telegram to the recently appointed U.S. Marshal Bob Howland to find out what the actual situation entailed. Howland replied "Everything quiet in Aurora. Four men to be hanged in fifteen minutes." Midday saw a throng of vigilantes march into the jail and without any interference hang them in front of onlookers.[33]

Even communities with law enforcement had problems with vigilante groups who felt that immediate and severe actions were preferable to the standard course and speed of the courts. In May of 1876, area cattlemen of Shackelford County, Texas had had enough with an organized band of horse thieves whose business territory ran from Fort Griffin to Fort Dodge. When they cornered four of the gang members, a fight ensued and two of the outlaws were killed outright and the survivors were hung "without delay." A fifth member of the gang, named Taught, was arrested by the marshal at Fort Griffin and placed in custody. "A few nights later a group of vigilantes took Taught from the jail, carried him to a place on the Clear Fork, and hung him to a tree. A card was pinned to his clothing with this inscription: *Horse Thief No. 5 that killed and scapled that boy for Indian sign. Shall horse-thieves rule this country? He will have company soon.*"[34] The frustration with the criminal justice system was heard clearly. A week later, a man wanted for horse theft in Eastland County was arrested in Fort Griffin.

Turned over to deputies to be transported back to Eastland County to stand trial, he was found hanging to a tree three miles out of Fort Griffin. In 1877 a man was taken into custody for the crime of rape and held in the jail at Georgetown, Colorado. Vigilantes entered the jail in the middle of the night, taking the jailers by surprise. The suspect was taken outside and lynched at the frame of a nearby building. The following morning this poem was found with the body and gives some insight to the actions of vigilantes:

Not a bark was heard, not a warning note,
As we o'er to the calaboose hurried;
Not a Thomas cat cleared his melodious throat
Where our hero in slumber lay buried.
We entered his cell at the dead of night,
The bolt with the jail keys turning,
The moon's pale crescent had sank out of sight,
And never a lamp was burning.
No useless stogas encased his feet;
And we saw, as we carefully bound him,
That he stood like a coward, dreading to meet
The shades of the victims around him.
Few and short were the prayers he said—
He did not have time to say long ones—
But he steadfastly gazed at the frame o'er his head
and grieved that the posts were such strong ones.
We thought, as we hoisted him up from the ground
And made the rope fast to a corner,
That the cool morning zephyrs would whisper around
A corpse without even a mourner.
Lightly they'll talk of the deed that is done,
And wonder, "Who was it that hung him?"
Though little they'll grieve to see him hang on
The beam where the "Vigilance" swung him.
As soon as our cheerful task was done,
Ere the light of the morning was firing
The peaks that glow in the rays of the sun,
We prudently spoke of retiring.

Sternly and gladly we looked on him there
As we thought of his deeds dark and evil;
We heaved not a sigh, and breathed not a prayer,
But we left him alone with the Devil.[35]

Power of the Press

The press of the Old West seemed, at times, to encourage individuals to take action into their own hands should law enforcement be absent. In the shooting death of Curley Walker, the *Abilene Chronicle* reported on July 13, 1871, "He was a great villain and 'his loss is our gain.' Let the work continue until the country is cleared of such thieves and cut throats as Curly Walker."[36] Curly Walker was already a known horse and cattle thief when he stole a herd of cattle from Captain Wemple and sold it at Fort Dodge. Wemple sent for a deputy marshal but before he arrived, Wemple felt Walker was preparing to leave. He confronted Walker and a gunfight ensued in which Wemple killed Walker with a shot through the heart. The press report clearly was a message not only condoning this particular action but calling for others to follow suit.

In June of 1880 the editor of the *Yellowstone Journal* wrote:

> The presence of horse thieves whether white or red is so apparent and their work so proven that it calls for some concerted action on the part of those most interested. Valuable animals are constantly disappearing and the losses incurred at this advanced portion of the season are irremediable. . . . And these predatory scoundrels are gathering fast. They have their organizations and . . . are desperate men. . . . They know they deserve to be strung up or shot down in short notice, and that when caught that method of disposing of them is usually resorted to. . . . While we are positively opposed to mob law except in the extremest [sic] cases, we are fully aware that something must be done for the protection of our property.[37]

In the summer of 1882 the *Yellowstone Journal* included the following editorial: "There appears to be a horse stealing boom throughout the territory, and if it doesn't collapse the organization of the old-time necktie festivals will be in order."[38] This was not just a phenomenon of the frontier press; in September 1935 the *Anti Theft Association News* (Vol. 34, no. 3, pp. 8) reprinted an article from the *Warsaw (Missouri) Times*, with the headline "Vigilantes Needed." Reporting a spike of chicken, horse, and cattle theft the article implies nothing; it calls for vigilante action and the creation of anti-theft organizations. "The farmers must for self protection organize 'vigilantes' committees for their own protection. Let Judge Lynch hold a few sessions of court and there will be a cessation of this thievery."

The *Republic County (Kansas) Journal* printed a more common account that some readers thought both condoned and condemned the actions of vigilantes against a suspected horse thief.

On the night of the 20th, near 2 o'clock, the team, wagon and harness belonging to Doc. Hancock, a brother of Mr. M. Hancock, of Scandia Tp., was stolen, and ran off. Quite a number started in pursuit, among them Wm. Stanley, who overtook the team, in possession of the thief, some 85 miles northeast of here [somewhere near Fairbury, Nebraska]. He immediately took possession of the team and thief by virtue of a navy six [revolver]. The thief examined Stanley's authority and found it was correct, therefore concluded to submit. Stanley brought him into Belleville last Friday night, and turned him over to the Under-Sheriff Latham, who brought him before a justice of the peace. Here he waived examination, but owned that he stole the horses. In default of bail he was committed to jail, to await trial at the next term of court.

He gave his name as Fritz Meier and also as Rankin; was evidently a German, was well dressed in a suit of gray, said his home was in Illinois, where he claimed to have a wife and three children, and was apparently about forty years of age.

During the night a mob attacked the jail, breaking down the outer door; but Latham managed to quiet them until he could run the thief off into the country, where he kept him until morning, when he lodged him in jail again. On Saturday evening the mob broke into the jail, took the prisoner out and down to the creek west of the city, hung him up on a sort of derrick, used by the butchers in dressing beeves [sic], where he was found Sunday morning. There is no doubt but that he was guilty of stealing the horses. There is no doubt but that he was a sneak thief—at any rate, he bore the marks of one. Still we do not believe the parties who were instrumental in the hanging did right. We have laws and men should abide by them. Two wrongs do not make a right. Myer [sic] stole the horses; the mob hung Myer. Myer outraged the law, but the mob did worse: they took the life of a human being.

We are a believer of lynch law, but only in the most extreme cases, and then only after a full, cool and careful investigation. There was not hot blood about this; it was a cool, premeditated job. They apparently went at it as deliberately as they would a day's work.

Now, we don't care how much Myer deserved this punishment, we are very, very sorry that there are people in Republic county who so far forgot themselves as to commit a lawless act of this sort. It will go with them down through their lives, and be ever present with them. It is no light thing to take a human life, cruelly, as this appears to have been done. It not only injures the parties who do the act, but it is a terrible example of lawlessness to set before the young who are to come after us. We have laws—let us obey them, and see that they are obeyed. It cannot be done by breaking them . . .[39]

With the large number of horses being stolen in Texas and taken either into Mexico or other states to be sold, the press got behind movements that encouraged the vigilante attitude. Consider the following editorial published on March 8, 1878 in the *Frontier Echo*:

It is estimated that 100,000 horses in Texas have been stolen within the last three years. It is further estimated that 750 men are regularly engaged in the business, and not over one in ten is ever captured and brought to justice. By common practice in rural districts every man caught is either shot on the spot or hung on the nearest tree. And no instance is yet recorded where the law paid the slightest attention to lynchers of this kind. It is concluded by judge and jury that the man who steals a horse in Texas forfeits his life to the owner. It is a game of life and death. Men will pursue these thieves for 500 miles, go any length, spend any amount of money, and fight them to death when overtaken. That they will be exterminated admits of no doubt. The poor scoundrels cannot last long when the feeling of our civilization is so much aroused against them as it now is in Texas.[40]

In 1876 the *McKinney Enquirer* reported on a petition that was being circulated in the area that was asking the Texas legislature to change the punishment system of horse theft to a sentencing guideline that included the whipping post for the first offense; whipping and branding for the second offense; and the punishment for the third offense, hanging. The *Frontier Echo* responded to the petition with the following retort:

Get out with your nonsense. What's the use of all that bother? Hang 'em first; then if they persist in their innocent amusement, cremate them. If that does not put the kibosh on 'em, we don't know what will.[41]

Another suggestion made to end horse thievery was the requirement of a test or expurgatory oath. Under this process a person could be denied certain privileges "unless he swears that he is not, never has been, and will not become a horse thief."[42] This particular oath expanded the definition of a horse thief to include not just the actual stealing but attempt, aiding in the theft, advocating, advising or teaching horse theft, and anyone who was affiliated with or a member of a horse-thief front. Popular with the press, which urged its adoption as practice even before it was codified, it eventually failed due to its compulsory self-incrimination.

The *Mineral Argus* published out of Maiden, Montana, was

reporting on the activities of Stuart's Stranglers, a vigilante committee formed to stop horse thievery in the mid-1880s. The paper "editorialized vigorously" the actions of the Stranglers: "The most speedy and safe cure is to hang them [horse thieves] as fast as captured." As the actions of the Stranglers continued, the number of horse thefts declined. One local rancher was quoted by a newspaper in Calgary, Alberta: "Some recently elected deputy sheriffs are raising a howl about it, but the general opinion is that as far as stock interests are concerned, the hanging was a great success."[43]

Home on the Range

Kansas of the Old West was a battle ground on so many fronts: free or slave state, Native American disputes over land, and corporate battles between the railroads and stage companies. Sometimes horse theft was used as a weapon. Caldwell, Kansas, saw vigilantes rise up against horse thieves and law enforcement as two stage companies vied for lucrative government contracts. In July of 1874 the county sheriff had just returned from the pursuit of horse thieves when he was ordered to go to Caldwell to serve warrants issued by the court for an organized horse-thief ring that had recently targeted the mules of Vail & Co. Concerned over the knowledge that many of those listed in the warrants were known to be dangerous, the sheriff called upon many persons from Wellington, Kansas, to assist in the serving of the warrants.

Getting close to the town of Caldwell, an advance scout was sent into town and came back reporting that most named in the warrants were armed and were planning to resist any attempt to take them into custody. The sheriff sent out a call for reinforcements and at two o'clock in the morning he entered town with 150 men and searched all residences of town until he affected the arrest of all those named in the warrants. A newspaper account of the action ended with speculation of what a trial would bring to light: "What the testimony will be we are not prepared nor at liberty to state; but our readers may be prepared for starting disclosures, and the presentation of an array of evidence that will prove the existence of an organized band of horse thieves extending all along the border. *The end is not yet.*[44] Nor was it, for the same paper later reported that at midnight a mob of armed men stormed the jail, overpowered the guards, and hung the three men being held in town. The three hung had interesting backgrounds: one was an ex-lawman, one a member of Sumner county bar, and one was believed to be the son of the ex-governor Edwards, of Illinois.

A.C. McLean, charged with being involved in the theft of mules in Caldwell, gave testimony that explained the process of the theft:

> When I first saw the stock it was in charge of Brooks and Granger. Granger told me that he was assisted in bringing the mules down by all the rest of the party. Granger also told me that they were going down to Kingfisher, to clean out the station (steal the mules) belonging to Vail and Co.; and that Charley Smith had been sent to Stinking creek to steal stock there. The party that went to Kingfisher, failed to get the mules there, because they were too well guarded by Al Needham and two men armed with needle guns. As they were returning to Kingfisher, they were attacked by Indians, and Bill Watkins, who had gone down to help steal the mules, was killed and scalped, and Granger's horse was shot. Bradbury, who kept the station for the Southwestern Stage Company at Stinking Creek, was to help Smith steal Vail & Co.'s stock at that place. Bradbury formerly lived near Caldwell.
>
> About the day before the Indians Attacked and killed Pat Hennessey, two of Vail & Co.'s drivers came to my ranch with the U.S. mail. They had a sulky and one horse. After they had passed a few hours the S.W. Stage came in. William Brandon was driving. Bill Brooks was on the stage. He (Brooks) told me that he intended to overtake and steal the horse belong to Vail & Co., that had passed down the road. Brandon and Brooks were both afraid of an attack by the Indians; so I

armed myself and drove the stage down to Baker's, twelve miles below. Brooks told me that they (the horse thieves) had taken the contract to run that mail line and that they intended to do it.

He said that they were employed by the South Western Stage Company to prevent Vail & Co. from fulfilling their mail contract, at all hazards; that they were to steal their stock and prevent, by any means, the transmission of the mails on the route from Caldwell to Fort Sill. That they (Brooks & Co.) were paid six hundred dollars by the South Western Stage Company for the clearing the road, i.e. stealing the stock and stopping the mails, the first time.[45]

The people who could prove the conspiracy, not with hearsay but with facts, were the three who happened to be left in Caldwell and were hung by the mob. Caldwell, Kansas, being so close to the Oklahoma Indian Territory and several major trails, remained a center of operations for horse thieves throughout the expansion era.

Butler County, Kansas, is a perfect case study of a vigilante response to horse thieves. In 1870 the area was fraught with reports of horse thefts. An editorial printed in the *Walnut Valley Times* April 29, 1870 stated: "There must be some horse thieves in Southwest Kansas. Numbers of horses are missing. Lynch law should be put in force."[46] A response was reported in the same paper in less than thirty days telling of two unidentified men found dead on the trail with the note "Beware of Horse Thieves" pinned to their bodies.

Stories appeared in print of the capture of five men (from a gang of nine) who were captured for stealing 127 government mules from a wagon train at Bluff Creek, Kansas. Those captured alive were taken to Arkansas to stand trial, but they escaped and returned to Butler County where the horse thefts continued. The frustration of the people was expressed in another editorial of the local paper: "The citizens of Little Walnut are organizing for mutual protection against horse thieves. It is proposed to make some of these fellows pull hemp without judge or jury. Hanging is the only effectual remedy for horse thieves, and the quicker the better."[47] Early fall saw three horses stolen from the cabin of a Butler County resident. Upon notification of the theft and the direction of travel by the thieves, the resident went out to get his horses. Three days later the recovery party returned with all three horses but no thieves. The only comment made was "Them thieves won't steal any more horses."[48] It was known and discussed by county residents that several organized horse-theft gangs were in operation. Known horse thieves were watched to learn of associates. The "mutual protection" group found stolen horses hidden away and would return them to the rightful owners.

The continuous and blatant theft of horses and the ineffective law enforcement response drove those wishing to form a mutual protection society to structure themselves along military lines (many were Civil War veterans) with the title of regulators. By late fall the regulators numbered in the hundreds and they had had enough. A family living near Wichita, who had recently been pistol whipped and had three teams of horses stolen, were in the Butler County town of Douglass when they saw one of the men who had attacked them. This was what the regulators were waiting for.

That night masked men of the regulators went to a home where they knew three of the thieves had gone. Forcing their way in, they ordered the surrender of a man named Corbin and the Booth brothers. With women and children in the home, the men surrendered. The regulators took the men by gun point to a nearby heavily timbered area and a rope was tied around the neck of Corbin. The regulators demanded to know the names of other horse thieves as they pull him off the ground then released him several times. Satisfied that they had a complete list, they pulled Corbin up for the last time, leaving him hanging. The Booth brothers pled to be shot. The regulators gave them a running start then dropped them in a hail of gunfire. A coconspirator was shot the same night with the note "Shot for a horse thief" pinned on his body.[49]

An inquest was held the following day and it was formally determined that the four men had died at the hands of unknown persons. Family members of the victims met with the sheriff and soon eighty-seven men and one woman were named in arrest warrants for the murders of the Booths. Obtaining the warrants proved much easier than serving them. The regulators took control of the town and all roads leading to it. The sheriff was turned away and four additional suspected horse thieves were held in a store.

By 1:00 a.m. on December 2, two hundred armed men took the four suspects south of town. Three confessed to involvement in a horse theft ring and named nearly one hundred others. Having heard enough, the regulators hung the four and faded into the night leaving four ornaments of frontier justice to greet the morning sun. Underneath the tree hanging these ornaments, was an unobstructed view of the town, for "underneath the norms of legal and institutional behavior in societies lies a great beast, the people's capability for outraged, uncontrolled, bitter, and bloody violence."[50] The light of day brought shame, guilt, and fear to the point that many left the area never to return.

The role of the vigilantes throughout history has almost always been vampiric in nature; exposed to the sunlight of public scrutiny, they seemed to die. Even the honest and innocent townspeople would engage in rituals and sport charms and signs in hopes that the men of night would spare them. Soon it was the anti-horse-thief societies, operating in the open as warriors of the light of justice that continued to fight the horse thief.

Chapter 5

The Thieves

The Routine Activities theory of crime states that crime will exist when there are potential victims, potential offenders, and lack of capable guardians. The horse, as the main mode of transportation, assured that there would be potential victims. The rapid expansion west and the corresponding delay in establishing governmental offices made law officers a scare resource. It is the third element of this theory, the thief, that has captured the imagination of so many. The following profiles explore the complexity and depth of the horse thief.

Doc Middleton

There may always be some debate about which team or player has the best record, but in the career of horse theft the recognized all-time slugger would have to be James "Doc" Middleton Riley. His undisputed claim of stealing 2,000 horses in two years earned him the title of "King of the Horse Thieves" and a spot in Buffalo Bill Cody's Wild West Show! Stealing his first horse at the age of fourteen, Doc Middleton also added other crimes to his resume, including murder. Convicted of murder in 1870 at the age of nineteen, he "was sentenced to life in Huntsville Prison. Four years later, Doc escaped from jail and fled to Nebraska by joining a cattle drive."[1]

In the ongoing Plains Indian Wars, Doc and his gang were found to be equal-opportunity thieves, stealing from the

Lakota and Sioux tribes and from the government herds stationed to fight the Native American tribes. Operating from the Dakota Territory to the Sandhills of Nebraska, Doc and his boys soon became the boogey men of stolen horses, with any horse stolen in the area being attributed to the Doc Middleton Gang. Enough thefts and public attention soon resulted in a special agent of the department of justice being ordered to track him down. The King of the Horse Thieves lost his crown on September 18, 1879 when he was sentenced to a five-year prison term on a guilty plea of grand larceny.

Ned Huddleston

Ned Huddleston, born a slave, found that the freedom that came with the end of the Civil War may have opened one door, but access to employment and community acceptance remained locked tight. After the Civil War Huddleston eventually found a job as a rodeo clown. This position did not pay well, placed him in constant physical danger, and was all at the amusement of the audience. Travelling the country with the rodeo, Huddleston developed a skill with horses that continued to grow. Not able to ride in the rodeo—what he really wanted to do—Huddleston developed few friendships, but while in Mexico he struck up an acquaintance with a young man named Terresa. Discouraged over lack of pay, Huddleston quit the rodeo and with Terresa started a business of their own—stealing horses. Huddleston and Terresa would steal horses in Mexico and drive them north of the border to Texas where they would be sold to unsuspecting cowboys and ranchers. Huddleston and Terresa drifted apart and he worked several jobs, including capturing and breaking wild horses. Huddleston quickly gained a reputation as "the best bronco rider that ever threw a leg over a horse."[2] With a growing reputation, bankroll, and self-esteem, Huddleston met, and quickly fell in love with, a Native American woman Tickup and her child fleeing her abusive husband.

Huddleston had deeply understood the impact of abuse and understood the impact it had on children.

Huddleston took to his "adopted" child as if she was his own. Many were amazed at how gentle and at ease he was with his and all children. Huddleston's life seemed to be going well until Tickup's abusive husband appeared. Outraged that his wife had taken up with another man, he surprised Huddleston, tied him up, and took Tickup, his daughter, and Huddleston's possessions and left. Tickup, suffering yet another beating from her husband, killed him in his sleep and fled the state.

Huddleston had started a slave, worked hard, entered a life of crime, gone straight, and started a family. In one night he had lost his fortune and his family, but not his resolve. On his horse he started his quest to locate Tickup and the child he so adored. Many months and hundreds of miles later Huddleston tracked her down only to find that she had taken another lover. All that had made sense to Huddleston and made his past trials bearable had again been taken from him. Dejected, he turned back to horse theft. In 1875 he joined the Tip Gault Gang which included his old friend Terresa.

In California the Tip Gault Gang ran into trouble stealing a string of horses and one of the members was killed. While Huddleston was digging the grave, the owners of the horses came calling; the ambush seemed complete but Ned survived by hiding in the grave with the body of his fellow gang member. Finding that the ranchers had left his gang members dead where they fell, Huddleston collected all of their money belts and with an influx of cash decided once again to go straight. His rebirth included a move to Oklahoma and the new name of Isom Dart. Life as a law abiding citizen proved dull and no amount of cash seemed to stop the nightmares. Soon Huddleston, now Dart, was back in his old haunts and soon a new gang was engaged in the wholesale theft of livestock in Wyoming. A warrant was issued for Dart and soon he was in the custody of deputy sheriff Joe Philbrick. On the way back to the jail, the buckboard wheel slipped, the horses were spooked, and down they fell into a small canyon. Philbrick was unconscious and injured while Dart was unscathed. Many outlaws on the way to jail, finding themselves suddenly free, would leave the injured deputy to fate, but it was not in the soul of Dart. Tending to the injuries, Dart got the buckboard back on the road with the deputy and drove to Rock Springs, where he deposited Philbrick at the hospital for professional care and turned himself in at the jail.

The trial of Dart saw deputy Philbrick testifying as a character witness after which "the jury, completely ignoring the cause for which the colored man was being tried, unanimously agreed that no man who had done what Isom had done was a menace to society, and forthwith turned him loose."[3] Once again Dart had been given another chance at a straight and honorable life, and this time he knew he would make it.

Dart started his own ranch breaking horses and trading them for cattle. Dart continued his reputation as a top-notch rider. Early area-pioneer, George Erhard said of Dart: "I have seen all the great riders, but for all-around skill as a cowman, Isom Dart was unexcelled and I never saw his peer."[4] Although Dart continued to remain friends with several of his past outlaw acquaintances, he never returned to the life of an outlaw.

While Isom was growing his herd, horse theft and cattle rustling had reached a peak in Wyoming and the cattlemen had hired Tom Horn to wipe out the theft problem once and for all. No one was safe from Horn and his campaign to eliminate anyone associated with cattle theft. Dart had a friend, Matt Rash, who was suspected to be a cattle thief. His friendship with Rash, and his previous reputation, made Dart, as well as Rush, a viable target and both were killed by Tom Horn. Born a slave on a farm in Arkansas as Ned Huddleston, Isom Dart was buried a free man on Cold Spring Mountain and mourned by many.

"Dirty" Dave Rudabaugh

The background of the successful horse thief and those who caught them often seemed the same. It has long been known that *it takes a thief to catch a thief,* and that held true in the case of horse thieves. Several of the famous and infamous law men of the Old West had a past that would not stand up to today's standards but in the frontier towns it would often be considered a bona fide occupational qualification. Consider the following case of "Dirty" Dave Rudabaugh.

Dave Rudabaugh, born in 1854, was a native of Illinois but moved to Eureka, Kansas. His trail to Kansas was like many others: his father died in the Civil War and his family moved from job to job and finally landed out West. While in Kansas, he earned the moniker "Dirty" Dave Rudabaugh and his reputation as a horse and cattle thief. Not only did Rudabaugh excel as a horse and cattle thief, but he had the distinction of being so averse to soap that his "signature odor-somehow offended even gunslingers of the West in the late 1800s."[5]

Dirty Dave tried his hand at a variety of legitimate jobs of the times: messenger, cowboy, freight driver—none of which held his interest for any length of time. Tired of respectable work, Dirty Dave soon turned to crime, including robbery, cattle rustling, and horse theft. In 1876 Dirty Dave ran a gang known simply as "the Trio" consisting of Dan Dement, Mike Roarke, and himself. This gang specialized in horse and cattle theft. Soon other toughs joined the outfit and by 1877 it was known as the Rudabaugh-Roarke Gang.

Having a tough time in the illicit livestock business, Dirty Dave and compatriots tried their hand at a new line. In 1878 Dirty Dave and friends robbed a train and was caught by a posse led by Bat Masterson out of Dodge City. Not looking forward to prison, Dirty Dave turned state's evidence. One paper reported that "Someone has said that there is a kind of honor among thieves. Rudabaugh don't think so."[6] With

the community temperament understood, a move was in
order and in what some saw as an attempt to go straight, he
became a policeman in Las Vegas, New Mexico Territory.
Rudebaugh's past was not held against him; on the contrary,
it seemed just what was needed in this wide open and wild
town. Unfortunately recidivism raised its ugly head as Dave
was recruited to join another criminal gang run by John
Webb, a Las Vegas lawman who was part of the posse that
caught Rudabaugh in Kansas.[7] Lesson not learned. He rode
with "Billy the Kid," ambushed Wyatt Earp in Arizona in
1882, and met his end in Mexico, beheaded, at Parral.[8]

Dutch Henry

Dutch Henry saw the West as a land of opportunity. The
geography of the Oklahoma Indian Territory and Colorado,
along with its jurisdictional disputes, made it prime real estate
for an organized horse-theft operation. Henry was believed
to control a horse-theft ring of three hundred criminals
operating between Vinta, Oklahoma Indian Territory, and
Pueblo, Colorado. The location of the present-day Oklahoma
Panhandle served as a clearing house for Henry's operation.
Horses stolen in Colorado would be exchanged with horses
stolen from the Oklahoma Indian Territory (and vice versa)
and the new horses would then be sold without fear of
identification. In 1877 soldiers from Fort Elliott caught nine
of his gang and hanged them all. Soon Henry was caught and
convicted of stealing government mules and sent to prison.
With the quick and constricting response of the soldiers from
Fort Elliot and the loss of their leader, the gang soon became
horse-thief history. In 1878 Henry was arrested in Trinidad,
Colorado, and taken to Dodge City, Kansas, by Sheriff Bat
Masterson to stand trial for horse stealing. That trial ended
in acquittal due to insufficient evidence, but it wasn't long
after that he was back in custody.

    In reporting the arrest of Dutch Henry in Trinidad the *Ford
County (Kansas) Globe* reported on January 7, 1879 that

"'Dutch Henry,' the man who seems to be wanted in different states and territories for a variety of crimes, such as horse-stealing, mail robbery, and even murder, and of whose arrest . . . was brought before Judge Walker to-day, upon complaint of Sheriff Wootton, that he is a fugitive from justice in Ford County, Mr. W.B. Masterson of Dodge City, was present as a witness." The newspaper further reported, "Dutch Henry is rather a genteel looking man for a horse-thief, road agent and murderer. He has black hair and eyes, black moustache, long face and Roman nose. His eyes are bright and penetrating, and indicate quick intelligence. He is dressed in a good suit of black, white shirt and other corresponding clothing."

"The appearance of Dutch Henry is that of an educated German-American, and his language is very slightly broken. His career open[ed] in the west in 1867, when he joined the Custar expedition, since which time he has been a roving plainsman. He says no one in the west knows what his real name is. . . . Parties who claim to know say that Henry's real name is Henry Borne."[8]

Dutch Henry was not without compassion and reason. Charles Goodnight, a rancher and leader of many who had moved to the Pandhandle, quickly heard of Henry and his operation. Goodnight hired a guide and located Henry and asked him to leave his settlement alone. He stated that his men were armed and would defend themselves, but if Henry promised to leave them alone they would do the same. Henry agreed and by all accounts both lived up to the bargain.

Flatnose Currie

Many famous outlaws, bank robbers, and killers started on their outlaw trail with horse theft. Flatnose Currie of the Wild Bunch was one such outlaw. Within the annals of the Old West there is no better-known outlaw gang than the Wild Bunch. The Wild Bunch had a somewhat fluid membership of about twenty-five, which included Flatnose Currie along with a much smaller core group. George Sutherland "Flatnose"

Currie was born on Prince Edward Island, Canada, around 1864 and as a young man moved to the Nebraska Territory with his family. Like so many outlaws of the Old West, Flatnose Currie started his criminal career stealing horses. The Sandhills of Nebraska were his primary stomping grounds, for the geography allowed for the hiding of horses and the evasion of the long arm of the law for those who knew their way through the maze of hills. Gaining a reputation of a skilled horse thief, Flatnose Currie met up with Kid Curry who, "coupled with the newcomers Butch Cassidy and the Sundance Kid, soon had Flatnose eyeing the cash stashed in the vaults of the region's banks."[9] Soon afterwards, rewards were posted for all members of the Wild Bunch, including Flatnose Currie. There were several reports of the demise of Flatnose Currie at the hands of lawmen and some report that after the break-up of the Wild Bunch, he lived out the remainder of life in Chadron, Nebraska, with a daughter. The exact circumstance of his death is unsure but his name and reputation continues in the legends of the Old West.

William H. Finch

William H. Finch was an African American post tailor at Fort Sill. Finch was not only known for his skills with a needle and thread but with the ladies as well. Discovering Finch climbing out the window of his daughter's bedroom, the post barber shot at Finch but missed. Finch was ordered off the post and Finch complied, stealing two handguns, a horse, saddle, and bridle. Two detachments were sent in pursuit but were unable to catch him. Two weeks later he was arrested and three soldiers appeared at the jail to escort him back to Fort Sill. The three-day trip back to the fort was interrupted on the second night when Finch killed two of the guards stealing both their guns and horses. Caught by a pursuing detachment of cavalry, he was taken in front of the infamous Judge Parker where he was tried and hanged.[10]

John Hunt Morgan

Horses were rare and valuable during the Civil War. Horse breeding and racing brought about some of the most notorious high-stakes thefts of the expansion era. Woodburn Farm of Kentucky was known as a leader in the 1860s of professional breeding of fine thoroughbreds. Alexander, the owner, was the first to print a catalog of horses and livestock for sale at auction. The area being fraught with horse thefts, Alexander felt he was safe being a British citizen and flying a British flag.[11] Alexander failed to realize that horse thieves, like the early American colonials, were not prone to give all deference to the British.

During the Civil War Woodburn Farm became the target of horse thieves. Horses were at a premium during the war and were often stolen to sell to the Union or Confederate representative buyers. Several persons rode into Woodburn Farm disguised as US soldiers, but some were soon recognized as thieves who had stolen horses from the farm before. Holding one Capt. Willa Viley captive, to serve as a guide, the column was in fact riders associated with William Clarke Quantrill. They invaded the house, fought with Alexander, and made off with fifteen thoroughbreds and trotters.[12]

Sometimes the label of horse thief or hero depended upon a person's allegiance in the war. John Hunt Morgan was a brigadier general, a cavalryman, and in the summer of 1863 went by the moniker of the "Thunderbolt of the Confederacy" and the "King of Horse Thieves." Morgan's raid through Indiana and Ohio with Federal Troops never more than a few hours behind him was legendary. He failed in his attempt to rally the Copperheads, Northern members of the Democratic Party that were against the war and arguing for armistice with the Confederacy, but he did manage to wreak damage to the infrastructure of Indiana and Ohio that "amounted to at least ten million dollars."[13] To avoid capture, Morgan and his troops would take horses along the way with no concern of where one's sympathies fell. As several Copperheads approached him to acknowledge their support, the following exchange took place: "'Good,' he is reported to have said to one of them, as he took the Copperhead's horse. 'Then you ought to be glad to contribute to the South.'"[14]

The Musgrove Gang

L.H. Musgrove of Denver, Colorado, was a prototypical organized crime leader who would not be out of place in present day. In charge of a criminal enterprise that not just committed robbery and murder but specialized in stealing horses in more than six states, he was described as "a man of large stature, of shapely physique, piercing eye, and steady nerve . . . a man of daring, inured to danger, calm at the most critical times—a commander whose orders must be obeyed, who planned with wisdom, and who executed with precision and dispatch."[15]

Musgrove's enterprise covered most of the frontier states with operations and agents located in Colorado, Kansas, Nebraska, New Mexico, Texas, and Wyoming where they engaged in the wholesale theft of horses and would move the stolen horses to different operations hundreds of miles away, where they could be safely sold and new stock stolen and returned to the state or territory from which they started. Musgrove would handpick a lieutenant for each area of operation who would be trained and supervised by Musgrove personally. Many of these lieutenants would go on to gain notoriety as outlaws in their own right, such as Ed Franklin and Sanford Duggan.

Musgrove led by example and often would engage in operations personally. In the operation that eventually led to his capture, Musgrove was being pursued with his stolen horses and mules by US Marshal Haskell. Finding a defensible place in Wyoming, Musgrove sent a flag of truce and a message to the marshal. The message said he could come in and pick out any stick he could recognize and leave, but he could have no more. The offer was accepted and Marshal Haskell realized that Musgrove indeed had the perfect spot and his capture would have to wait to another time and location. Musgrove was finally captured and returned to Denver for trial while horse owners throughout the West celebrated!

The Williams Brothers

Ed and Lon Maxwell, known under the aliases of the Williams brothers, fell under the spell of the James brothers and decided that crime was the way to advance in the post-Civil War country. Although they worked with the James brothers, they were never part of the gang for they decided to specialize in horse theft. Their area of operations spanned five states: Illinois, Wisconsin, Minnesota, Nebraska, and Montana. They quickly became known as experts in eluding the law and used several tricks on the stolen horses, such as getting whiskey up the noses of the horses to stop them from making noise as pursuers approached. They both were caught and did time in prison but after their release the lure of quick money was too strong. Deputies made an attempt to arrest the pair who had returned to horse theft, which led to a shooting and the death of two deputies. They were caught near Grand Island, Nebraska, and during their preliminary hearing a mob of several hundred stormed the courtroom, pulled them outside, hung them, and dispersed. Their reign of crime, like so many horse thieves before and after, ended on a limb of a tree.[17]

No Arm Jack

Dallas, Texas, had a visit from a singular character—Jack Hall, alias No Arm Jack—en route to Stephenville jail, from which institution the prisoner escaped six months ago after receiving a sentence of ten years in the penitentiary for horse-stealing. Both his arms are off above the elbow, having been crushed in a sugar mill when he was a child, but the bones grew out several inches from the flesh, and their surfaces are rough like corncobs, and Jack writes a beautiful hand by holding a pen beside his chin and pressing the protruding bone against it. He shoots a pistol or firearms expertly, and manages a horse as well as the average two-handed man. The height of his ambition appears to have been stealing horses successfully. He is about thirty years of age. He was arrested in the Choctaw Nation.

—*Marion (Ohio) Daily Star*, August 14, 1882[17]

Shep Tinker

A story published on June 27, 1880 in the *New York Times* illustrates how the labeling theory came to create the criminal career of Shep Tinker and his gang of horse thieves. Born in Putnam, Ohio, in 1810 he moved with his family to Perry County where he grew up with a long history of mischief. In 1830 a farmer had a horse stolen from a barn and Tinker was the primary suspect. Drunk in a tavern, Tinker created a grand account of his theft when pressed. He was then quickly charged, convicted, and sentenced to prison. Evidence then came to light that proved Tinker could not have committed the crime, that his story was nothing more than drunken bragging. Upon his release he once again stated that he was never a horse thief but since the court and area-people branded him as such, they should start protecting their stock. In four years he created a gang of thieves that operated, with accomplices, in every county in Ohio.

After several years in the "horse business," he expanded to counterfeiting and was promptly caught. Considered handsome and blessed with the gift of gab he plied his "gifts" on a local girl who fell in love with him, stole the jail keys from the sheriff, and released Tinker. Gone for ten years, his gang continued operation. Tinker returned in 1855 reporting that his delay was due to visiting the penal institutions in Illinois, Indiana, Iowa, and Wisconsin. He told all who would listen that he was reformed and was willing to be elected as justice of the peace. Having his offer turned down, he rejoined the gang and started his old life by robbing the county judge of his horse, followed by a forced removal of a traveling clergyman's horse. Caught again, he was sentenced to ten years and pardoned after five. He made another offer to be justice of the peace with the campaign promise to drive the horse thieves out of the state. He won the election but was disqualified to serve. He did disband the gang, spending the rest of his days on a small farm. Tinker stated that his gang had stolen more than 4,000 horses while they were in operation.

JERSEY VIGILANTES TO ACT
Anti-Horse Thief Society Decides Now to Protect Women, Too.
Special to The New York Times

TRENTON, N.J., March 3. Stirred by the Allison murder at Moorestown . . . the Consolidated Vigilant Society of New Jersey and Pennsylvania, in annual session here today, decided by a unanimous vote to amend its constitution . . . extending its scope beyond the mere pursuit and apprehension of horse thieves, its original purpose.

We were organized to protect horses," declared one of the members, "but now we intend to protect women from the criminals that have for so long been a menace to them, especially on the lonely farms in the country districts."

—Published March 4, 1906

Belle Starr

Belle Starr was born in 1848 near Carthage, Missouri. Having moved to Texas with her family, Starr met Cole Younger, who is believed to have fathered her first child. This union did not last and Starr became romantically involved with another outlaw, Jim Reed, who gave Starr a son. In 1869 Starr and Reed made their living robbing and rustling in the Dallas area where Starr became known as the "Bandit Queen." Crime, as an occupation, is not without its hazards. In 1874 Starr's husband was killed by one of his gang members. Leaving her children with her mother,

Starr did what any self-respecting horse thief would do—she moved to the Oklahoma Indian Territory where she led her own gang of horse thieves. The Sans Bois Mountains proved to be lonely and Belle Starr soon began living with Sam Starr, a horse thief in his own right.

Belle and Sam finally met the long arm of the law. Belle continued her notoriety, becoming the first female ever tried for a major crime by the infamous "Hanging Judge" Isaac Parker. In the case that ended her in front of Judge Parker, Belle stole a horse that belonged to a poor crippled boy—a case of horse theft that had other horse thieves urging her to return the horse.[19] After five months in federal prison, Belle and Sam were released and they returned to the Indian Territory and their previous occupation of stealing horses. In 1886 Sam was killed in a gunfight and replaced quickly by Belle with a member of the Creek Nation named Jim July. Caught stealing, Jim was headed to court and Belle was headed home. On February 3, 1889 on her forty-third birthday, Belle was shot and killed. No one was arrested, but the list of suspects included Jim July, her son Ed Reed, and even the brother of a former lover.[20]

WELLDRESSED WOMEN ARE STEALING HORSES AND RIGS

Several Buggies Left Standing on Streets Have Been Driven Away by Brace of Fair Horse Thieves.

Two women, whose descriptions have been furnished the police, are stealing horses and buggies left standing by their owners in the business section of the city. Yesterday afternoon about 3 o'clock the women were seen driving away from Austin's real estate office on Broadway in a buggy, belonging to E.O. Johnson of the Kentucky stables. The rig is still missing and the authorities have been unable to learn of its whereabouts or who the two women thieves are. The women are stout and welldressed. Both are dark complexioned and one is thought to be of Spanish descent. The stolen horse is a sorrel, with one white ankle. The buggy is a business vehicle, with a black body and red running gear. It has rubber tires. The police believe that the women have been implicated in the theft of several buggies and thus far they have been able to successfully elude the strong arm of the law. (Oakland, California, 1907)[21]

Burt Martin

It was the stare from Burt Martin that caused most to back down. Words did not have to be used when Martin stared behind the gun. A number of people along the Kansas-Nebraska boarder fell victim to a horse thief who made many feel that they came close to the end of the trail. Soon area law enforcement was on the lookout for the small man who so effectively relived people of their horses. Burt Martin was tried, convicted, and sentenced to three years in the Nebraska penitentiary for horse stealing. Eleven months into his sentence, it was discovered that Burt Martin was, in fact, Lena Martin. Dressed in man's garb, Lena told officials that she was Burt, a name she had used for some time. All assumed that Burt was an accomplished horse thief with a delicate constitution—a young man of nineteen. The discovery was made when guards heard inmates talking about Martin. A prison physician was called in and the "discovery of her sex" was revealed. Governor Savage released her from prison upon her "pledge to reform."[22]

Birdie McCarty

If you were a woman horse thief in Kansas, and got caught, it would behoove you to stay proficient in your prayers and scriptures, particularly in Judge Simons' court in Fort Scott, Kansas. The following story comes from the *A.H.T.A. Weekly News,* May 22, 1902:

Horsethief Could Not Pray.

A dispatch from Ft. Scott has this: Birdie McCarty, the notorious female horse thief, who was convicted at this term of court, gave away a year of liberty this afternoon because she was unable to repeat the Lord's prayer in court. Today was sentence day, and Judge Simons gave her five years. Previous to this the court asked her if she knew the Lord's prayer, and she said she did. "Now if you will repeat the Lord's prayer I will knock off a year of this sentence," the court said. The daring woman was trapped; she could not do it, and the judgment of the court stood.

What happened to Birdie McCarty should not imply that horse thieves were without religious desires. In 1767 the Anglican cleric Charles Woodmason happened to ride into an ambush of horse thieves in the South Carolina Back Country. Quickly realizing who they had captured, the thieves requested a sermon, which he agreed to do, upon his release the following Monday. Woodmason held true to his word and returned the following Monday along with a choir of militia. "The outlaws learned of this, and when Woodmason came to preach, the men speedily 'moved off-leaving their Wives, Whores and Children' behind them."[23]

Men or women, war heroes or thieves, the history of the west is crowded with people who tried to make a living out of stealing horses. The gender or cause may differ but in each case, once a person chose horse theft he could count on the law to pursue him.

Chapter 6

The Good Guys

The tracking and apprehension of horse thieves involved a process of reading the social and cultural signs as much as reading the physical evidence (tracking) of western lore. Some of the best "riders" were those who had some firsthand experience in the trade and therefore were well versed in the culture and thought-process of those they pursued. Throughout history, others recognize the benefit of an experienced enforcement force, such as Napoleon's creation of the Sûerté (criminal investigative bureau of the Paris Police) that included a convicted bandit as its first chief. The concept is a simple one: who better to catch a thief than one who used to be a thief!

Mysterious Dave Mather

Mysterious Dave Mather was a personality who could easily fit into a chapter on thieves or law men. In 1879 he was identified as operating with the horse thief Dutch Henry in Colorado and suspected (but not convicted) of assisting in an attempted train robbery with Dirty Dave Rudebaugh. The next year finds Mather in Las Vegas, New Mexico, as an officer of the law. In an effort to quell mob violence between two feuding groups the *Las Vegas Daily Optic* reported that Mysterious Dave Mather faced off against an armed man.

Instead of complying with his request, Castello suddenly pointed his murderous weapon at Dave Mather, and with a cocked pistol in his hand, threatened to shoot the officer if he advanced another step. Dave only knew his duty and knew the consequences that would result from a delay of action, so he advanced, and in the twinkling of an eye, almost before the breathless bystanders had time to see a movement on his part, he drew his trusty revolver from its place and fired one shot at the determined man, the ball taking effect in Castello's left side below the ribs, penetrating the lung, and ranging downward, passing through the stomach and liver.[1]

Within eleven months of reporting this daring exploit, the *Las Vegas Daily Optic* reported: "The friends who assisted in the escape are the dreaded gang of 'killers' who infested Las Vegas last winter . . . Dave Rudabaugh [Rudebaugh], 'Mysterious Dave,' 'Little Allen,' . . . are known to be the most desperate men on the plains."[2] Three years after this account Mather is reported as thwarting a jail break in Dodge City, Kansas as a town marshal. From Dodge City or Kiowa, Kansas, Mather was reported as an effective lawman in the detection and apprehension of cattle and horse thieves, due in a large part to his personal experience.

William (Bill) Brooks

Another interesting lawman who rode both sides of the fence was Bill Brooks. Bill Brooks was a tough lawman and stagecoach driver who could always be counted on when most would fold up and leave. This could be an asset for a lawman and horse thief alike. The June 14, 1872 edition of the *Wichita City Eagle* reported one such example that occurred when Brooks was marshal of Newton, Kansas.

As near as we can get the facts, the Texas men were on a spree, and, as a consequence, making it hot for pedestrians. Brooks had run them out of the town, when they turned and fired three shots into him, with what effect may be judged, from the fact that he continued his pursuit for ten miles before he returned to have his wounds dressed . . . Bill has sand enough to beat the hour-glass that tries to run him out.

Two years later Brooks was captured as one of a gang of mule thieves in Caldwell, Kansas, and hung with two others by a group of vigilantes (*see Chapter 4*). "The bodies were hanging facing south. Hasbrouck was on the left, Brooks in the center and Smith to the right and nearest to the tree. The distorted features of Brooks gave evidence of a horrible struggle with death."[3]

Jack Bridges

Jack Bridges gained a solid reputation in western Kansas as a deputy US marshal, bringing all sorts of criminals to justice, including horse thieves. Some placed Bridges in the "killer-class" of lawmen, but none would argue that he was ineffective when fighting the criminal element. Bridges was sworn in as the city marshal of Dodge City on July 8, 1882. His appointment caused many citizens, good and bad, to reminisce on the Ledford shooting. A newspaper account stated: "Early settlers remember Ledford, the chief of a gang of horse thieves, counterfeiters and desperados that traversed the wild regions of Kansas, the Indian Territory and the Panhandle. Jack Bridges, City Marshal of Dodge City, at that time was Deputy U.S. Marshal. He caused the breaking up and arrest of the gang, and in the capture of Ledford a desperate encounter took place . . ."[4]

John E. "Jack" Ledford ran a syndicated ring of horse thieves who operated with an organized method: "horses or mules stolen in one vicinity could swiftly be moved, usually by night, and hidden on ranches of affiliated members in a different location. Being so widespread and well-organized contributed to its success in confounding both military and civil authorities."[5] One of the tricks of Ledford's League was to dress like Native Americans when raiding a herd of horses to ensure that if seen, blame and the law would be turned elsewhere. Ledford's success ended with U.S. Marshal Bridges. Sometimes a tough reputation was the best job qualifier. Bridges was so feared by the members of Ledford's

League that they even made attempts to assassinate Bridges, who stayed the course until the gang was broken up.

General David J. Cook

Consider the Pinkerton National Detective Agency, founded in 1850, which brought the term "private investigator" into vocabulary. The very term implies the private nature of the work, which on occasion would be kept private for the ability to engage in extralegal activities in response to crime. The use of informants, reformed criminals, and even those still in the business as well as "enhanced interrogation" of suspects and witnesses, if known, would not be tolerated by mainstream society for long. The concepts developed by the Pinkerton Detective Agency were needed in the western frontier and they were adapted to the West by Gen. David J. Cook.

Gen. David J. Cook was the organizer of the Rocky Mountain Detective Association. Born in Laporte County, Indiana, in 1840, Cook moved to Colorado in 1863 where he worked as a government detective in 1864. Cook was elected sheriff of Arapahoe County in 1869 and continued working in law enforcement, as sheriff and deputy U.S. marshal through 1880. Cook was a major general for the Colorado militia and headed up the actions to end the Leadville Riots and Chinese Riots of 1880.

The crowning achievement of General Cook was the Rocky Mountain Detective Association. Communication between Old West agencies was poor, as was training on police procedure. "The Association was a non-government, mutual-assistance league of sheriffs, police chiefs, and marshals throughout the western states and northern Mexico."[6]

In 1866 when Cook was elected marshal of Denver, he posted a notice with the bold statement that if a citizen had stock stolen and reported it within twenty-fours of discovery, Cook would recover it or pay for it himself. He didn't have long to wait when a well-known area ranchman reported the theft of some of his prize horses. Pursuit led to the Boulder area but the trail ran cold. Upon his return to Denver, Cook found a message waiting from one of the members of his Rocky Mountain Detective Association indicating that the horse thieves were headed for Kansas. Cook gave pursuit and was able to arrest his suspects and prove the worth of his detective association.

Wyatt Earp

Wyatt Earp, of Tombstone, Arizona, fame, served as a lawman in several western towns, bringing many horse thieves to justice. In May of 1875, for the monthly salary of $60.00, Wyatt was a policeman in Wichita, Kansas where his first arrest was reported in the *Weekly Beacon*:

> On Tuesday evening of last week [May 4], policeman Erp, [sic] in his rounds ran across a chap whose general appearance and get up answered to a description given of one W.W. Compton, who was said to have stolen two horses and a mule from the vicinity of Le Roy, in Coffey county. Erp took him in tow, and inquired his name. He gave it as "Jones." This didn't satisfy the officer, who took Mr. Jones into the Gold Room, on Douglass avenue, in order that he might fully examine him by lamp light. Mr. Jones not liking the looks of things, lit out, running to the rear of Denison's stables. Erp fired one shot across his poop deck to bring him to, to use a naughty-cal phrase, and just as he did so, the man cast anchor near a clothes line, hauled down his colors and surrendered without firing a gun. The officer laid hold of him before he could recover his feet for another run, and taking him to the jail placed him in the keeping of the sheriff. On the way "Jones" acknowledged that he was the man wanted. . . . A black horse and a buggy was found at one of the feed stables, where Compton had left them. After stealing stock from Coffey county, he went to Independence, where he traded them for a buggy, stole the black horse and came to this place.[7]

It didn't take long for the reputation of Wyatt Earp and his brothers to grow. Earp was one of the few well known lawmen and gunfighters of the Old West to live a long life and die of natural causes.

Battled with Horse Thieves in Oklahoma

Sheriff A.J. Bullard and Undersheriff Cogburn, of Roger, Mills county, Ok., were killed Monday afternoon in a battle with horse thieves while the officers were attempting to arrest members of the band of outlaws. The fight occurred in the northeast portion of the county and continued for about 30 minutes, the outlaws finally surrounding the two officers and riddling them with bullets. The entire band made its escape, supposedly uninjured although the sheriff's posse put up a plucky fight. Bullard had served two years as sheriff of that county and was recently nominated by the Democrats for re-election. While it is not positively known who composed the gang of outlaws, yet suspicion points to the Burt Casey band as they have been operating in that portion of the territory.

—*Anti-Horse Thief Weekly News*,
Published July 3, 1902

Bat Masterson

Bat Masterson came to Kansas in 1872 and started work on a buffalo hunt. In 1874 Masterson signed on as a civilian scout in an Indian Territory expedition that led to the famous battle of Adobe Walls in the Texas Panhandle. His reputation as a man who would stand his ground, Masterson returned to Kansas where he served a variety of law enforcement positions. Masterson gained a reputation as a lawman who could catch horse thieves, often with just good detective skills. In early 1878, as sheriff of Ford County (Dodge City), Masterson was informed of the theft of horses, which he quickly deduced was committed by James McDuff. Collecting his evidence and the testimony of an arrested accomplice, Masterson travelled to Las Animas and made his arrest.

On March 23, 1878 a man came to Dodge City and reported he had two horses stolen from him last December. Armed with a description of the horses, Masterson started a search and soon recovered one of the two horses. April 17 the same year, four men came to town searching for four horses stolen the day before. The horses were soon found without the thieves and the owners left town happy. Masterson continued the investigation until two men were arrested for the thefts. May 18 found Masterson arresting a horse thief but unable to recover the stolen horse. *The Dodge City Times* reported "Horse thieves find hospital reception at the hands of Sheriff Masterson. He is an excellent 'catch' and is earning a State reputation."[8]

Although the legend of Bat Masterson is today associated with gun battles, it was his consistent and relentless pursuit of horse thieves that gained him the respect of the people in the West. In 1879, upon hearing of the arrest of the famous horse thief Dutch Henry, Masterson travelled to Trinidad, Colorado, to question him and attempt to return him to Kansas to answer many charges there. Horse thieves could be beaten but politics eventually proved to be an enemy that drove Masterson first to Colorado and then to New York, where he lived out his days as a sports writer.

USED A TROLLY CAR TO CATCH HORSE THIEF

Hammond (Ind.) Policeman Displays Both Daring and Rare Presence of Mind.

Special to The New York Times.

HAMMOND, Ind., July 6.—A sensational capture of a horse thief was made by means of a Hammond, Whitney and East Chicago trolley car at 3 o'clock this morning in the loneliest part of the city. A telephone message was received from Chicago announcing that a man with a horse and carriage, which was stolen, was headed this way from South Chicago. . . . Elsner ordered him to stop, but the man lashed his steed into a gallop. The policeman fired several shots after him, the bullets going through the carriage cover. Then Elsner rushed into the car barns and took a car out single handed.

. . . and after a chase of several miles came upon the thief and the horse and buggy. . . . Officer Elsner took him back to Hammond, and he was bound over to the Lake Superior Court in heavy bonds for horse stealing. He pleaded guilty to the charge. (Published July 7, 1903)

Presidents

Tennessee was not going to let Kentucky become the state known for horse breeding and racing without a fight, and who better to lead the fight than Andrew Jackson. Before becoming president of the United States, Andrew Jackson founded a racecourse near Nashville. On May 30, 1806, Andrew Jackson shot and killed Charles Dickinson in a duel. Dickinson, a rival horse breeder, accused Jackson of reneging on a horse race bet and called his wife (Rachel) a bigamist. Jackson, known for his temper, challenged Dickinson to a duel. Jackson received a shot to the chest and then shot and killed Dickinson.[9] Having clearly shown his love of horses, Jackson as president saw horse theft, and crime in general, a problem in the expanding western frontier and "approved the use of vigilante methods of Iowa pioneers, pending the clarification of their territorial status."[10] Jackson was not the only president who condoned vigilante action.

Theodore Roosevelt, while ranching in North Dakota, "begged to be admitted to a vigilante band that was being formed to deal with rustlers and horse thieves."[11] He was denied admittance to the group but did have the opportunity to track down some horse thieves. In his 1888 book about ranch life, Roosevelt reported that horse theft was a major issue and that every rancher had to be on guard against the crime. One winter, a boat Roosevelt and other members of the ranch had left on the bank to cross the Little Missouri River was stolen by three men suspected of being horse thieves. Because it was winter, pursuit by horse along the banks of the river was not practical and ranch hands experienced in such matters constructed a boat that would allow pursuit.

Dodging the ice flows and camping in freezing conditions as they went down-river, the trip on its own, was a major feat of skill and daring. On the third day downriver, they spotted the stolen boat.

"We had come to the camp of the thieves. As I glanced at the faces of my two followers I was struck by the grim, eager look in their eyes. Our overcoats were off in a second, and after exchanging a few muttered words, the boat was hastily and silently shoved towards the bank. As soon as it touched the shore ice I leaped out and ran up behind a clump of bushes, so as to cover the landing of the others, who had made the boat fast."[12] The capture was made without a fight but the problem of what to do with the thieves quickly came to the forefront. It was more than a week before the rescue party encountered another person. They made their way to a ranch and then Roosevelt took the captured men to the nearest town where, "Under the laws of Dakota I received my fees as a deputy sheriff for making three arrests, and also mileage for the three hundred odd miles gone over—a total of fifty dollars."[13] A big stick may help international politics, but in the plains of the Old West, a colt worked just fine.

Gun Notches

Contrary to the portrayal of western movies, there were really "few, if any, [people] engaged in bounty hunting as a full time vocation."[14] Rewards could encourage some, on occasion, to join a posse or dabble in bounty hunting. Take the case of Bill Dunn who had on his list of experiences that of cattle rustler, rancher, law officer, and the occasional bounty hunter. Recognizing opportunity when it literally knocks on the door, on May 2, 1895 Bill and a brother shot and killed Charley Pierce and Bitter Creek Newcomb who had stabled their horses in Dunn's barn. They collected a $5,000 reward after taking the bodies to Guthrie, Oklahoma. There is also the case of a criminal, soldier, buffalo hunter, and bounty hunter named Andrew "Buckshot" Roberts. Buckshot "attempted to collect the reward offered for outlaws who sought *him* for the death of rancher John Tunstall. Roberts was killed in the gunfight that ensued at Blazer's Mill, New Mexico, on 4 April 1878."[15]

In the western frontier, hospitality was expected, not just for the sake of good manners, but for survival as well. Cabins in the mountains or any area prone to cold weather and snow were always left with the fireplace perpared to start a quick fire. Travelers caught in the weather could find refuge in a nearby cabin, and when leaving they would reset the fireplace and replace any stores used or leave payment with a note. The camp fire on the cattle trail was the same. Travelers could expect to be welcomed and the sharing of a meal was often assumed. This hospitality, on occasion, was abused and often the job of profiling visitors fell upon the cook.

Two former cowboys from a ranch stopped by a camp with some very handsome horses. The cook wrote "I learned they had five 'wet' horses they'd picked up in Texas. In the fall they went to Kansas, supposedly to shuck corn. They'd spot several horses, then wind up their work and leave; soon they'd return unbeknownst and get the horses, and on the way south they'd drop in on my camp. I finally told them a Kansas man had been looking for them, and they quit coming my way."[16] Hospitality was expected, horse thieves were not.

In 1877 a group of Mexicans planned to start a freight line to deliver supplies in the Tascosa area of Texas. A gang of horse thieves stole all the horses and mules being used to haul the freight. While law enforcement gathered a description of the outlaws and horses, the burgeoning businessmen took jobs at local ranches to raise money for a new team. Their interference with a supply train hurt all legitimate ranchers and left little sympathy for the thieves. Several weeks after the theft, a leader of the gang rode into a ranch riding one of the stolen horses pretending that he was hunting a job. The rancher declined but stated that he could take him to a larger ranch where they were hiring, knowing that this ranch was where the horses' rightful owners were working and the hands were well-armed. Approaching the ranch, the "guide" gave a nod and the man was captured, confessed to where the gang was located, and confessed their future plans of murder and theft. He was turned over to the owners who promptly hung him.[17]

Claim jumping was a very real problem in the western frontier and it was in the forefront of many minds during the Oklahoma land rush. Evan Barnard and his friend Ranicky Bill, with a few other cowboys, gathered together in 1889 to secure their land claims. Following the law and staking a claim often was not enough to hold the claim. "Private force clearly was both a necessary supplement to, and a substitute for, legal right." More than once Barnard had to use force and the threat of force to hold his claim. The use of force for legitimate claims led to resentment and soon Ranicky Bill was accused of horse theft, which resulted in a visit from vigilantes. Ranicky Bill escaped and surrendered to authorities to clear his name. The vigilantes then threatened Barnard and his friends, lifting one neighbor off the ground with a noose twice. He refused to confess and Ranicky Bill was cleared of all allegations of horse theft, which incited the entire neighborhood to take up arms "against the vigilantes, who ceased their operations."[18]

John Abercrombie, also known as John Robinson, and Bronco John, was a horse thief who was caught, tried, convicted, and sentenced to prison who deserves a mention not because of his crimes but because of his humanitarian actions. The US Jail at Fort Smith in the mid-1880s was a facility that lacked any resemblance to the jails of today. Rats outnumbered inmates and proper sanitation would require the skills Hercules used in cleaning the Augean Stables. In 1886 an epidemic broke out in the jail and Bronco stepped forward to act as a nurse for the inmates. Working day and night offering aid to the suffering inmates, Bronco developed pneumonia and died in March of the same year.[19] Even horse thieves have need of a doctor.

In 1905, young doctor Urling Coe moved to Bend, Oregon, seeking adventure and he was not disappointed. It was a warm February day with heavy rains and flooding in the range when a horseman approached a ranch that had the last telephone on the line and called out to have them telephone the doctor. He stated that there was a hurt man in what was believed to be a deserted homestead some eighty-five miles from town. With no other explanation he turned his horse and rode off.

Coe was called and decided he had no choice but to respond. His plan was to take a team and buggy to the ranch, which would be half-way to the location of the injured man. The forty-five mile ride took all night due to the poor road conditions. Arriving at the ranch with the telephone, the owner explained that it was probably "Some of that goddam bunch of high desert hoss thieves." He also stated that if it was not for the flooding on the ranch "I'd like to ride over there with you and pot a couple of the damn wallopers."[20]

Coe was given a fresh horse to which he attached his saddle bags filled with equipment to handle most medical emergencies. After getting directions to the remote homestead (at the base of a butte) some forty miles away, he took off. As Coe travelled, the weather started to turn cold as he came to a river swollen with the flood waters from the recent thaw. In crossing the river he kept his saddle bags dry but little else. With his matches ruined by the water and the coming winter storm, he decided to press on. The snow seemed to increase at the same rate the temperature dropped, and he soon realized he was in trouble. Just as he realized he was close to freezing to death, he saw the outline of a corral then passed out.

Coe woke in a cabin housing several men who worked for Grizzly Colton, a man suspected of running a gang of horse thieves. Colton drew the doctor's attention to "Tex," one of his "employees." Tex had been shot twice with one wound in his leg seriously infected. When asked how it happen, Colton replied "he must'a been in front of the bygod gun when tha damn thing went off, I reckon. But that part of it ain't none of your goddam business, Doc. I got ya out here ta fix tha boys up pronto so's we kin git ta hell out'a here, an' that's all in Chrise world ya got ta worry 'bout, ceptin ta keep yer goddam mouth shet plumb tight from right now on. If ya keep yer goddam mouth shet 'bout it ya'll git yer pay fer it some day, but if ya ever let a yap ou'a yer face ya won't never need no bygod money. Savvy?"[21]

Coe agreed and performed a difficult but successful operation on Tex in the cabin. Coe also patched up several others who had seemed to be on the wrong side of some sort of confrontation. Coe keep his word and returned to the ranch with the story that the man had died and they left with the body before he arrived. That summer, Coe saw a man from the cabin who rode up to him and gave him a bag filled with the payment that had been agreed upon. Coe got his payment and his adventure, and eventually Grizzly got caught and sent to prison. Coe visited Grizzly in jail and learned that it was their plan to kill him after he treated Tex so he could never tell what he saw. They had decided that anyone who would make the trip in such weather had to be alright, and they let him live.

THEY STILL HATE HORSE THIEVES

Middletown, N.Y., Jan. 12—The oldest anti-horse thief association in the country, the Mount Hope Vigilant Society for the Detection of Horse Thieves, has held its seventy-second annual meeting. . . . for since the day of its organization not one of its members has had a horse stolen.

During the war of 1812 and for some time after peace was declared horses were very scarce. Thieves were active and successful. They flourished . . . and their work was carried on by a well-organized band, which was greatly assisted by a number of well-to-do residents of the district who contrived to shield and protect the regular thieves for the consideration of a share in the proceeds. . . . So successful were the pursuers that in every case the stolen horses were recovered, and in several the thieves were captured. These vigorous measures soon broke up the band, but the society still lives and prospers.

—*New York Times,* January 13, 1889

Many lawmen, citizens, and people from all walks of life found that they needed to stand up to horse thieves. It took great courage, and for some, great sacrifice. As the frontier moved west, many recalled the societies of the east that brought people together in the common cause of the detection and apprehension of horse thieves. Homer (850 B.C.) stated, "Union gives strength, even to weak men." In the west, union soon came in the name of the Anti-Horse Thief Association.

Chapter 7

Rise of the Anti-Horse Thief Association

The Anti-Horse Thief Association, as a multi-state fraternal organization, is a direct descendent of similar societies in the 1700s. "The primary objective of the earliest vigilants was the horse"[1] and the organizations all shared a similar structure. Geography, war, economics, demographics, and cultural changes are the common ingredients in the recipe of these covenant groups. Anti-horse-thief societies in general fall in the middle of a continuum, which has at one end the extralegal violent vigilante groups and at the other end the normative behavior of little-to-no citizen involvement in law enforcement. A close look into the largest of the anti-horse-thief societies, the Anti-Horse Thief Association (A.H.T.A.), provides an opportunity to better understand not just this organization, but the phenomena in general.

In the northeast corner of the state of Missouri, where the Des Moines River joins the Mississippi River, the states of Iowa, Illinois, and Missouri come to a point—a point that in the mid 1860s proved to be an epicenter for horse theft. Heavily forested valleys and deep ravines allowed thieves to hide as they prepared to cross one of three state lines into a jurisdiction that would provide some safety from pursuers. "The A.H.T.A. was born out of necessity. At the close of the war thieves and robbers were thick in Missouri and the officers of the law could not cope with them. Something had to be done to protect the people, and the A.H.T.A. was organized."[2] In recounting the conditions that led to the creation of the A.H.T.A. one settler offered the following account:

> But there were scores of organized thieves who followed stealing for a business. They would steal anything, no matter whether it was loose or not . . . The territory selected by these bands of organized thieves to operate in was an ideal one. It was that of northeast Missouri, southeastern Iowa, and that part of western Illinois lying immediately east of the territory just mentioned. . . . Thieves are like foxes, they must have their regular crossings. In the territory in question on the Des Moines River, there were seven crossings. On the Mississippi River there were four crossings that were used by thieves. . . . A horse could be stolen and before daylight they would have him out of the state. . . . Something had to be done in the way of protection or go out of business. Neighbors would counsel together, and after considerable deliberation a few vigilant committees were appointed, but for lack of organization the desired result was not obtained.[3]

The Civil War also contributed to the creation of the A.H.T.A. in several important ways. The demand for horses for the war created a black market that enticed many to enter the trade of horse theft to supply both sides of the war effort. Because many males of qualifying age had joined or were drafted into service, many farms and small communities were left with few men who normally would have taken on formal or informal policing roles. This vacuum of capable guardians made many potential offenders sit up and take notice. The end of the war, when the A.H.T.A. was formed, saw many veterans returning home with no jobs and possessing skills that made horse theft a viable option for quick cash. The flip side saw veterans who were willing to stand and defend what was theirs and to organize in quasi-military units to protect the property of friends and neighbors. Vigilante groups had risen from time to time in the area to address issues of crime, but they had lacked structure and the organizational skills of a strong leader.

Maj. David McKee

Maj. David McKee has long been credited as the driving force in the creation of the Anti-Horse Thief Association as an independent and then national organization. The A.H.T.A. was not the first group to consolidate several independent anti-horse-thief societies. In 1880 the Newtown (Pennsylvania) Reliance Company brought together many like-minded societies including "delegates from thirty-odd companies, including six located in New Jersey and three in Delaware."[4] Soon the United Company of Pennsylvania was formed (1821) and in 1891 "an association composed of societies in New Jersey and Pennsylvania got underway."[5]

Maj. David McKee was born in Illinois on December 14, 1823. His parents were frontier farmers from Kentucky and Pennsylvania, who married in Kentucky where they farmed until 1815. They then moved to Indiana and later permanently settled in Illinois. It is likely that one or both of Major McKee's parents were familiar with one of the many anti-horse-thief societies that existed in Pennsylvania and Kentucky. McKee's father died when David was ten years old and he stayed on the farm with his mother until the age of eighteen, when he married Martha Keescker and moved to Iowa to farm. In 1848 the McKees moved to Clark County, Missouri, where Major McKee remained until his death. Martha died in 1855 and the following year he married Mrs. Elvira Breeding. Major McKee had seven children by his first wife and twelve by his second wife.

Major McKee's service started in June 1861 when he enlisted as a private in the 1st Regiment, N.E. Mo., Home Guards. On June 11, the same year, he was elected 2nd lieutenant of a cavalry company commanded by Capt. D.F. Hull. On July 4 he was elected major of the same unit. Later that month, after several skirmishes, he was ordered to St. Louis where he was promised to become major if he helped raise a battalion of cavalry, which he did. McKee described his service from that point on:

The Battalion was known as the Black Hawk Cavalry and was under the command of William Bishop. Myself being the Major, I was mustered in by Captain Smith, U.S.A., at Alexandria, Mo., sometime about the 15th of November, 1861. My Command arrived in Macon City on the 27th of November where I remained until the 7th of May, 1862, continually on active duty, frequently commanding the post, but most of the time scouting in the field. During this time had a number of skirmishes with bushwackers, bridgeburners and the most noted of which was the fight at Crabapple Orchard in Boon County, Mo. I surprised with my party, the enemy at daybreak, killing and wounding between 20 or 30 and taking 33 prisoners and 61 horses and mules.[6]

His unit was merged with the Seventh Missouri Cavalry Volunteers and in July of 1863 he was honorably discharged due to wounds and returned home. It was later that year that he formed the Anti-Horse Thief Association. W.E. Spilman reports that McKee actually started the Anti-Horse Thief Association in 1854 after returning from a trip to California. ". . . He called a meeting of his friends together at the Highland school house in Jefferson Township, Clark County," Missouri, and organized the first A.H.T.A. of which he was elected the first president. From this first group, other similar organizations sprang up. However, because of their imperfect system of secret work, and the coming of the Civil War, the organization was not very effective. "The term 'secret work' referred to the signs, grips, passwords and other devices by which members identified one another and kept their meetings and activities concealed from outsiders. Presumably what happened was that this information had fallen into the hands of non-members, who were using it for their own advantage."[7] This became a recurrent theme in the reconstituted A.H.T.A. as members were constantly told to know their secret work, and to keep it secret. Returning from the war in 1863, because of disability, McKee reorganized the A.H.T.A., "with the imperfections corrected, as we now have the organization."[8] Although it is quite possible that McKee started an earlier anti-horse-thief society, (there are several examples of anti-horse-thief societies that used the term "Anti Horse Thief Association" in their title that pre-date the A.H.T.A. and should not be confused with the national fraternal order discussed in this chapter) the majority of historical accounts set the origin date clearly as 1863.

> Every member should keep well posted in the secret work of the order. He does not know when he may need it.
> —*Anti-Horse Thief Weekly News,* May 8, 1902

Major McKee proved himself a most capable horse-thief detective, willing to track down thieves for some distance and even disguising himself to affect a capture. On one trip, McKee tracked a horse thief to Iowa and captured him, knowing that the thief had the reputation of being a dangerous man. He handcuffed the prisoner to himself and on the return trip to Athens, Missouri, arrived too late to turn him in to authorities so he kept the man chained to him at his home. Upon awakening, his children did not recognize him and were very alarmed finding two "strangers" chained together in their home. This experienced proved to be valuable in the organization of the A.H.T.A. but did not place him in high regard in the criminal community.

In 1860 there were concerns of foul play over the disappearance of a man named Whitford. A search was conducted in which Major McKee found Whitford's body and determined he was murdered. A man named Baird, who had a long record of acts of violence with his gang, was convicted and hung for this murder. Baird, and nefarious people like him, had no use for McKee. Major McKee and his family lived in a sturdy brick home, and on several occasions he had to barricade the doors and use his rifle to persuade intruders to leave. Before he was eventually hung, Baird and company attempted to gain access to the McKee home one night but the Major had bolted and barricaded the doors as soon as their presence was detected. After a failed attempt to use fence rails as a battering ram, they tried to ambush McKee shortly thereafter when he traveled in the woods. Not one to run away from a fight, McKee "made such a show of resistance with his ever ready rifle that they sulked away."[9] It seems that it was providence that placed Maj. David McKee, a man with military experience, organizational skills, and a history of catching horse thieves, into a part of Missouri that was plagued with a criminal element bent on getting rich from the theft of the ever-important tool of the frontier, the horse. McKee proved to be the right man, in the right place, at the right time.

The Birth of the Anti-Horse Thief Association

Major David McKee called a meeting in September of 1863 at Luray, Missouri, with the expressed purpose of creating the Anti-Horse Thief Association. Present at this meeting were James Day, David Mauch, Maj. David McKee, H.L. McKee, David Shular, and John Wilson of Clark County; Wm. Beach, William Everhart, S. Grant, Jonathan Longfellow, and W. Matlock of Scotland County; and Jas. McGowen of Upton, Iowa.[10] The men called were well known in their communities and were looked upon as civic leaders. H.L. McKee was Major McKee's brother and a successful area farmer, having served in several county offices. "Daniel Shular was one of the oldest residents of the county and had owned farms and traded along the Mississippi as far south as New Orleans. William Everhart was a prosperous merchant. . . . It would seem that the founders of the AHTA were the same community leaders who took active part in other protective associations."[11] These men drafted a constitution and by-laws and advertised the next meeting in October.

The location of the second meeting seems to be in dispute. Several articles and personal accounts list the second meeting being held at Millport, in Knox County. (Several first-person accounts like that of John Fortune, who claimed to be a charter member of one of the first four sub-orders, list Millport as the site of the second meeting. Like the starting date of 1865, these accounts do not correspond to primary source documents and were probably influenced by the constant reporting of Millport and 1865 in various public addresses and as reported in the *Anti-Horse Thief Weekly News*.) Nolan points out that the original records of the meeting show that instead of Millport, it was held in Athens, Clark County, on October 23, 1863. This is further supported when one considers that the Athens location would have been much closer to the home of Major McKee.

The second meeting held in Athens included persons from Clark, Knox, Lewis, and Scotland counties in Missouri and Davis, Lee, and Van Buren counties in Iowa. A constitution and by-laws were approved, which created a grand order and a number of sub-orders. The officers elected to the grand order were Maj. David McKee, grand worthy president; John Grant, grand worthy vice president; Jacob S. Bennington, grand worthy secretary; Hiram Beach, grand worthy treasurer; Henry L. McKee, grand worthy marshal. The slate of officers differs from most historical reports apparently coming from an address made to the Iowa Grand Lodge in 1887 by B.R. Vale; however, the slate of officers reported comes from the original records, which even includes the total of votes for each person nominated for the office.

The preamble to the first Constitution adopted in 1863 is not very unique in the annals of anti-horse-thief societies. The preamble reads:

> Whereas, We the citizens of North East Missouri having suffered so long from theft committed by horse thieves and burglars that we consider it our only safeguard to bind ourselves together for the preservation of our persons and property, and we call upon all honest men to join us in putting down and bringing those rogues to suffered the penalty of the civil law.[12]

Compare the preamble of the A.H.T.A. to the preamble to the constitution of the Brush Valley Association for the Detection and Apprehension of Horse Thieves adopted a decade earlier in 1853:

> We the undersigned citizens whose names are annexed believing in the importance of an associated effort for the prevention and arrestation of horse stealing and being desirous of forming a society to shield us from its evils and afford Mutual assistance in case of loss by theft, do herby agree to form ourselves into a society, for the purpose of concentrating our efforts on this object, and do herby adopt the following rules and regulations for our Government.[13]

The constitution of the Scottville, Illinois Horse Thief Detecting Society (also known as the Mt. Zion Self Protective Society) had a preamble that very closely resembled that of the A.H.T.A.

> We whose names are annexed, desirous of forming a society to protect each one of us from the evils and losses attendant upon Horse Stealing and other Robbery, do pledge ourselves to be governed by the following Constitution and By-Laws.[14]

Formally established with a constitution, the Grand Order of the Anti-Horse Thief Association of Missouri and adjoining states began operations and the process of working out many of the organizational issues faced by any new grass roots organization. To be effective within their communities the A.H.T.A. not only had to be successful in the return of stolen horses and the capture of the thieves, but they also had to be seen as a viable and legitimate asset to the community.

Symbols of Legitimacy

To ensure acceptance by the communities, the Grand Order of the Anti-Horse Thief Association of Missouri and Adjoining States established an internal system that mimicked the courts in their functioning. The first constitution called for a vigilance committee whose job was to detect and apprehend the suspected horse thief and then to review the evidence to determine if a *prima facie* case existed and, if so, to turn the suspect over to the proper authorities.

This committee shall consist of six members of this society. It shall be their duty when a person or persons have been arrested and handed over to them charged with theft, they may investigate the case and if they think there is sufficient cause to found a prosecution they shall hand them over to the civil law, attending personally and with assistance and influence of the society to their legal prosecution. They shall have power to call legal advice when necessary.

It shall consist of two separate and distinct committees, and shall be designated as No. 1 and No. 2.

Committee No. 1 shall consist of ten or more members which shall be appointed by the president. It shall be their duty when directed by the president to hunt two days diligently for the trail of the thief, but if sooner found one of the party report immediately and the other pursue on.

Committee No. 2 shall consist of the owner of the stolen property and two other members and more if necessary, selected by the president, whose duty it shall be to follow the thief after his route has been discovered as long as any trail can be found and if caught it shall be their duty to hand him over to the vigilance committee.[15]

This concept remained important throughout the various modifications made to the constitution. Although the name "Vigilance Committee" was dropped, the later investigating and pursuing committees kept the same basic functions.

A later major personality in the Anti-Horse Thief Association, W.W. Graves authored the book *Law for Criminal Catchers* in 1906 that was used as a handbook for members of the A.H.T.A. on the legal issues they might face in the performance of their duties. Some of the topics included arrest with and without a warrant, use of force in arrests, breaking doors, rights of the accused, and the elements required for various crimes that members could make arrests for while in pursuit of horse thieves. Consider the following passage where one Judge C.A. McNeill gives advice on making an arrest without a warrant by a private citizen:

> If a felony, that is, a crime punishable by death or imprisonment in the state prison, is committed in the presence of a private citizen, it is not only his right but it is his duty to apprehend and arrest the felon, and such private person has the same right to arrest, for the purpose of preventing any person from committing a felony. It is also true that where a felony has been committed, although not in the presence of a private citizen, such private citizen may yet arrest one whom he has reasonable grounds to believe committed the crime.[16]

In addition to their procedure in the apprehension of criminals, the groups gained legitimacy through the ritual involved in initiation and granting charters. Membership was limited to men twenty-one years of age or older and admittance required a two-thirds vote of the members. Men of high character or standing in the community, who were members, assured the community that the association could be trusted. There are no records of how many persons were denied membership but the 1887 constitution included the following: "Any candidate having been blackballed, and afterwards removing to another locality, it shall be the duty of the W.S. of the Order in which said candidate was black balled to notify by private letter the W.P. of said locality of the fact."[17] This phrase suggests that some membership applications were rejected, and this revision assured that men could not go shopping for a chapter that would allow them membership. The same procedure is seen in many anti-horse thief societies. The Central Protective Association required reporting rejected candidates to the central organization: "If the applicative is rejected the Secretary shall immediately notify the Secretary of the Central Protective Association, and he shall notify all subordinate Associations, and said application cannot be presented again for six months."[18]

Once the appropriate members were selected, the identification of members became important, particularly for the riders in pursuit of stolen horses who needed to identify themselves to each other at a distance so as not to be mistaken for suspects. These long distance signs changed throughout the years, from "raise hat from head, give two circles and place back. Answer: same sign" to "three honks of the horn. Answer: two honks" when automobiles became the primary method of transportation. (The same source indicated that the oral distress or warning sign was "Hello, Major" and for the "Lady of the House" the distress or warning was to be "Do you know Major McKee?" clearly an homage to the founder of the A.H.T.A.) The night greeting became "three flashes of the headlights. Answer: two flashes."[19] When crossing jurisdictions, or in seeking the help of other lodges, the ultimate symbol of authority and legitimacy—badges— were used. Often worn on the inside of a coat lapel (so it would be hidden, and shown simply by lifting one's lapel), badges were common with many anti-horse thief societies and varied in shape and size as much as the badges of today. Also common were pin-back buttons, watch fobs, and other decorations worn as a visible symbol of membership.

Through the method and process of granting charters, and the accompanying certificate that was proudly displayed in the meeting hall or location used by the society, the sub-orders gained their own legitimacy. "The charter showed an American flag and an eagle, as well as the AHTA emblem. The form is of some interest:"[20]

To all to whom these shall come, Greeting: Know ye that we, the Grand Order of the Anti-Horse Thief Association of the State of Missouri and adjoining States do grant unto _____ and their associates this charter, constituting them and order to be known as Order No. ____ to be located at _____.

Know Ye, that this charter gives them and their associates, that may become regular members of the order, full power to receive persons into the order; also gives them full power to make such by-laws as they can agree upon, provided same do not conflict with the constitution and rules of the Grand Order. Also gives them power to send representatives to this Grand Order.

In witness whereof, we have caused this Charter to be signed by the Grand Worthy President and Grand Worthy Secretary, and the seal of the Grand Order affixed thereto.

For some communities the meeting location for the A.H.T.A. would be a common meeting hall for the community and this impressive document, displayed on the wall would act not just as a symbol of legitimacy but also as a recruiting tool. In the history of Vanderville, Illinois, the first town building was described as a multipurpose building, including the post office and general store. The second floor housed a doctor, barber, boxing ring, the Anti-Thief Lodge (referring to the A.H.T.A. which later became known as the A.T.A.) and a general meeting place.[21] Seen as a legitimate organization that met a need, the A.H.T.A. quickly started to grow.

ORGANIZE AN A.H.T.A.

The A.H.T.A. Weekly News, June 27, 1907

The A.H.T.A. means Anti-Horse Thief Association. In every sense of the word, however, it means anti-theft association. A thief is a thief to this association whether he has stolen groceries from the farmer's wagon on Saturday afternoon, chickens from the farmer's hen house at night or horses from his barn.

Catch 'em is the watch word of the order and they generally do it, the thieves have more fear of this association and less confidence in their ability to get away from it than from the officers of the law.

If there is any organizing done in Kansas, let it be branches of this association and less. If crops happen to be rather short, as it looks likely, the thieves will be on the move this fall and winter. If anything makes a man hot under the collar it is to have his chicken house invaded and a large part of the flock taken but warmth of feeling is turned to satisfaction when the thief has been caught and is behind bars. The object of the A.H.T.A. is to accomplish this and the records show they accomplish it nine times out of ten.

—*Topeka Mail and Breeze*

Growth in the Early Years

Major McKee served as president the first ten years (1863-73) and was replaced by his brother Henry. Growth blossomed in the original tri-state area due to in a great part the effectiveness of the association. There are not many specific accounts on record of the early days, but the annual reports indicate that they were called out on a regular basis and with success. A later account from 1902 provides an indication of why people might want to join and/or support the A.H.T.A.

In early 1902 the Allen family of Elm City, Kansas (close to the Oklahoma Indian Territory Boarder in S.E. Kansas) were gone from their farm when a hired hand, John Hahn, stole a revolver, some jewelry, and other personal items and then left with one of the Allens' horses. The Allens returned in mid-afternoon and after discovering the theft notified the local chapter of the A.H.T.A. A pursuit team of twelve members was established and started out after the thief. Early evening the next day, Hahn was caught in a hotel at Lenapath, Indian Territory. The pursuit team's investigation retrieved all but one of the stolen items, along with evidence in the form of receipts to ensure a conviction. With the recovered items and evidence "the prisoner was set astride the stolen horse and made to ride it back to Elm City. There he was put in the hands of Deputy Sheriff A.A. King, who, accompanied by Ed Allen and J.C. Vance, brought him to Chetopa [the county seat] Wednesday evening, where he was placed under arrest and bound over in the district court . . ."[22] The criminal was reported, caught across the state line, returned, and items were recovered within twenty-four hours. This case was the fifth that the Rose Hill lodge of the A.H.T.A. responded to and in every case the thief was captured.

Growth of the Anti-Horse Thief Association: 1871-1880[23]

Year	Number of Sub-Orders	Number of Members
1864	4	Not Given
1871	21	627
1873	18	571
1875	40	1,176
1876	64	1,932
1877	96	2,370
1878	113	2,720
1880	176	4,042
1885	184	4,973
1890	253	7,059
1900	379	10,191
1910	1,051	35,738
1912	1,113	41,685

During the annual meeting in October of 1881, the association agreed to establish state jurisdictions, resulting in greater expansion of the association. "This was one of the most important meetings in the history of the order,"[24] for there had been some internal debate over the group's organizational structure and resulting expenses that many felt were slowing the growth of the association. In his address to the members during the annual meeting, President Suter outlined the reasons the A.H.T.A. needed to move to state jurisdictions:

> The subject of State or District organization has particularly attracted my attention since our meeting last year. An intimate knowledge of the workings of the order has served to impress me with the necessity of State Organizations. The expense incidental to a full representation from the

subordinate orders in distant states is too great to be borne by many of them. No matter where the Grand Order might meet, this would be true. . . . I do not wish to be understood as desiring to sever the relations which at present exist between the various sections where the order is flourishing; on the contrary my desire is to connect them more firmly together and make the work better understood and more effective among those who are too remote to meet with us in the sessions of the Grand Order.

I see no reason why, with State grand bodies, represented by delegates in a National order, we may not all work together for mutual good in our noble cause. This is an institution which can be made instrumental in breaking the great army of criminals in the land. To do this we must organize subordinate orders in every state, and have intimate communication with each other. Orders retatched [*sic*] from each other amount to nothing. After the commission of a crime, the depredators do not remain in the vicinity of their lawless act, but flee to other and more congenial localities. Then it is that we need the assistance of our bretheren everywhere, whose aims and objects are the same as our own.[25]

The membership was swayed and state charters were organized, allowing for rapid growth in Kansas, Nebraska, and the Oklahoma Indian Territory. By 1916 the states with chapters included Arkansas, Colorado, Illinois, Iowa, Kansas, Missouri, Nebraska, New Mexico, Oklahoma, Texas, and Wyoming with membership approaching 50,000. The majority of these states, once state orders were firmly in place, would ensure that they were chartered under the laws of the respective states, many of which already had laws authorizing protective associations.

Not a Vigilance Committee

Not all groups that addressed horse thieves were vigilante organizations. Many, although private, still limited their activities to the detection and apprehension of the horse thief. Once caught they would turn the suspect over to the public authorities who they recognized as responsible for holding trials, and if the suspects were found guilty, the public authorities would pass sentence, including incarceration or death. This attitude grew when the populace felt that they could trust the law and order functions of the government— that law enforcement and the courts would not only be able to suppress crime but do so as blind as lady justice, impervious to the influences of the community elite. "Nineteenth-century Americans held onto the belief that a vigilant citizenry— rather than a standing army—was the best means to cope with social disorder. . . . This preference for regulation by citizen action rather than active public policing was shared by the antitheft societies. While they often complained that thieves escaped 'from the hand of justice,' they never lobbied state legislators for enlarged constabularies or a state police. Instead, they maintained that thievery 'requires the utmost exertions of every good citizen.'"[26] The largest anti-horse thief society, the interstate fraternal Anti-Horse Thief Association continued to call upon members to expand its chapters and authority, eventually changing its name to the Anti-Theft Association—never calling for commiserate increases in law enforcement during its existence.

The anti-horse-thief societies varied from vigilante groups in several ways. First, members had to pay fees to join, with additional assessments needed to continue their status as a member in good standing. This ensured protection to the members only and acted as a visible inducement for non-members to join. It was not uncommon, in the recovery of a member's stolen horses, to find additional stolen horses not belonging to members. These would be returned to the owners, if known, and law enforcement if not, which also became a great advertisement to join.

In a second important difference from vigilante groups, when suspects were captured they were turned over to legitimate law enforcement. In the Fourth Annual Session of the Kansas Grand Order of the Anti-Horse Thief Association, the grand worthy president in his address showed his concern that the association not be considered a vigilante group:

> In order that our Association may retain its high position in the estimation of those who are familiar with its aims and objects, it is necessary that the members conduct the affairs of the organization in such a manner as will convince the most skeptical that our aim is to protect property rights by seeing the statutory provisions concerning such matters rigidly enforced, and by our numbers and thorough organization we will be in a position to terrorize the transgressor to that extent that the A.H.T.A. will be as much a prevention as a cure. By the acts of the individual members the world at large will judge whether we are the offshoot of the organized mobs that the early settlers of the West have reason to remember so well, or an institution composed of the very best elements of the communities in which it exists.
>
> In all of the past year there has been reported to me but one act of violence committed by the Antis in pursuit of stolen property. That one case resulted in the death of a horse thief. The necessity of such a course was so apparent that the authorities deemed it unnecessary to hold an inquest, and even complimented the members on the orderly manner in which they had conducted the entire pursuit and capture.
>
> While I would admonish all members to refrain from all violence I do advise that when it becomes necessary to make an arrest of parties in possession of your property do so, let the cost be what it may. After effecting a capture, it is advisable that the investigating committee be represented by one or more members at the time of the trial, that the law may be honestly administered, for it is well known that in this day and age money is often a very potent factor in criminal prosecutions. As has been said by an eminent editor, "A little credit more, judiciously applied, will make most consciences as pliable as wax." The mere presence of the committee may and will prevent a miscarriage of justice.

Anti-horse-thief societies also differed from vigilante groups in that their organizations tended to last much

longer, often seeking to have their societies incorporated into
state law. These societies also served as a social group for
members; as several organizations found, once they formed,
horse theft dropped and members were never pressed into
service. These societies/chapters ended up spending more
time planning their annual gala than strategizing how to
respond to reported thefts. Vigilante groups typically had a
relatively short life span, formed when the problem arose and
fading away when their mission was accomplished. Certainly
this was the case in Montana with Stuart's Stranglers.

In the 1880s there was a gang known as the Missouri
badlands company whose criminal enterprises spanned
the territories of Dakota, Montana, and Wyoming as well as
extending into southern Canada. The stolen item of choice
was horses, because they could be moved quickly, handled
easily, and were very marketable. The gang typically raided
quickly and at night, moving the horses to one of many
secret or hidden canyons where they would attempt to alter
the appearance of the animal. The stolen horses would then
be transported to a territory different from one in which
it was stolen, to be sold to an unsuspecting buyer. During
the spring 1884 meeting of the Montana Stock-growers'
Association direct action was called for to stop the growing
horse and cattle thefts. Granville Stuart called for calm and
cool consideration and stressed that lynch law was not an
appropriate response.

In what was considered a failure to take action during
this spring 1884 meeting, the outlaws took the association's
response as encouragement to continue their looting. As
the ranchers began spring roundup, they left their ranches
to the outlaws who swept the country taking all horses left
behind. Stuart then called for a meeting that resulted in
the formation of a fourteen-member committee known as
Stuart's Stranglers. Trees all over the territory were found
to be bearing the fruit of horse thieves, so known from the
label placed on the coat of those hung. In July, a shootout

with horse thieves ensued where several were killed when the cabin they were in was set ablaze. Several thieves escaped the fire and were caught by Indian police. A deputy US marshal recruited a posse that included members of the Stranglers and arrived to obtain the thieves. The marshal's posse returned, reporting that they were overpowered by masked men who took the prisoners and hung and burned them. By the time these actions became well reported, the vigilante group had dissolved.[27]

In the story of George "W" Newton, author Usher Burdick states that Newton knew many leaders of the "Montana Stranglers" (so named because of their propensity for hanging) and that the organization was, in fact, led by "the biggest horse thief in Montana." Newton recalls how the organization hung one Eddie Bronson, the son of Major Bronson of Fort Buford, who may have been guilty of being an alcoholic but was not a horse thief. Years later when the victim's mother wrote the Montana Livestock Association asking what they had done with her son, the reply simply stated that "he had gone the route that all good horse thieves go."[28]

The reportedly indiscriminate hangings continued when the Stranglers hung a ferryman and his two sons because they were "assisting" horse thieves by allowing them to cross on their ferry. As they crossed the country in search of more horse thieves to hang, the Stranglers would seize any supplies needed, butcher cattle, and demand lodging, telling the owners to bill the Montana Live Stock Association, which of course never paid. Led by the "outlaw character" known as "Flopping Bill," they continued to hang men, some of whom were deemed horse thieves by general consensus. Newton suggests that hanging was not the exclusive method of dispatching assumed criminals. Newton told the story of how the Stranglers, numbering eighteen, were seen with two "half breed" prisoners. "Just what was done with these prisoners is not definitely known, although the same two men were found chained together in the bottom of a lake

in the vicinity of the Dog Den Hills, Dakota."[29] The actions
of the Stranglers seemed to be condoned by the livestock
association as long as horse theft went down.

There were several organizations clearly involved in
extralegal activities who did not consider themselves
a negative force. "Members of claims clubs, vigilantes,
and whitecaps, of course, proclaimed their allegiance to
community norms and saw themselves as establishing order,
not contributing to disorder."[30] Sometimes these groups
would butt heads with each other and usually it was strength
and organization that would determine who came out on
top. The A.H.T.A. is one such organization.

In all of the written materials and constitutions of the
order, great pains are made to ensure the public and remind
the members that the A.H.T.A. is not a vigilance committee.
Their motto, "Protect the innocent; bring the guilty to
justice," is defined as turning the suspects over to the proper
authorities. One such reminder appeared in the July 31,
1902 issue of the *A.H.T.A. Weekly News*.

> The Anti-Horse Thief Association bears no resemblance
> to the old time "vigilance committees," "regulators" or
> "whitecaps." It is just as much opposed to the methods of
> such bands as it is to thieving. . . . It has systematic methods
> of capturing those who deprive its members of their property
> rights . . . turns its captives over to the regularly elected
> officers of the law . . . employ no methods in carrying out
> the work of the order that cannot be readily endorsed by any
> good citizen, minister or court of justice.[31]

That is not to say there was never the occasional lapse in
judgment by members; such cases were carefully reviewed
by the order. In his address to the Kansas delegates at the
1885 meeting of the Fourth Annual Session of the Kansas
Grand Order of the Anti-Horse Thief Association, Grand
Worthy President Ed Corson told of a case by a state lodge
where a horse thief was killed in the pursuit of the stolen

horse. "The necessity of such course was so apparent that the authorities deemed it unnecessary to hold an inquest, and even complimented the members on the orderly manner in which they had conducted the entire pursuit and capture. While I would admonish all members to refrain from all violence I do advise that when it becomes necessary to make an arrest of parties in possession of your property do so, let the cost be what it may."[32]

There is an interesting case from Iowa in 1884 that is peppered with the suggestion of vigilante actions taken by members of the Anti-Horse Thief Association. In *Johnson v. Miller et al.* a trial was held in the district court of Black Hawk. The defendants were members of the Anti-Horse Thief Association and had voted to prosecute Johnson. Johnson took them to court for malicious prosecution and the jury found in favor of Johnson. When the case was appealed to the Supreme Court of Iowa, the finding of the district court was reversed. The reversal cleared the members of the A.H.T.A. although several issues came up that suggested the members were not opposed to conduct not publically sanctioned by the A.H.T.A. After the first indictment against Johnson was quashed, it became well known that the court was planning to quash the second. A few days prior to the court date, a letter was found near Johnson's house with a rope. The letter suggested that Johnson either take the indictment or move west. This letter was signed "We The Committee." A few days after acquittal of the criminal charges, Johnson's barn and contents were burned. One person stated that he heard one of the defendant's say "we will convict Johnson sure, or, if we do not convict him, we will drive him out of the country." Another testified that he heard an unidentified member state that if they were unable to get rid of Johnson any other way they would burn him out. The court ruled that there was not sufficient evidence to tie any of the threats or the barn burning to the A.H.T.A.[33]

Lynch law, although a common practice of some anti-horse-thief societies, was not the normative action for the Anti-Horse Thief Association. One report of very early action of the association suggests that the early members did not always heed the principles set forth. In the fall of 1863, the Mt. Pleasant area had suffered a number of horse thefts. Determined to end this practice, a number of members tracked the stolen horses to the farm of a man named Luzatter who had rented an area farm a year earlier. Luzatter was taken to a nearby town for an informal trial in which neighbors decided that he should hang unless he named all members of the gang of thieves, which Luzatter was initially unwilling to do. They continued questioning him while tying a rope around his neck and raising him from the floor and back down again. This interrogation method seemed much more effective, for Luzatter immediately told the group the location of the thieves and he was then released. A committee was quickly formed to go after the thieves and a week later, upon their return, any questions about the disposition of the other thieves was met with silence. "Mt. Pleasant was never bothered again with horse thieves."[34]

Fifty-five years later, in 1918 Burrton, Kansas, events played out that showed how the Anti-Horse Thief Association had matured and held steadfast to their principles. The U.S. was involved in World War I against Germany and in the Burrton area there were Mennonite families who by faith opposed war and supported nonresistance and had a strong German heritage. Buying War Bonds soon became something akin to a loyalty test and contributions to organizations such as the Red Cross were not enough to appease some members of the community. On November 11, 1918 "patriotic citizens" of Burrton decided the time had arrived for a showdown with the Mennonites. Five cars loaded with these citizens drove to the Schrag farm to force Schrag to attend the Armistice Day celebrations in Burrton. They forced their way into the Schrag home and removed him to Burrton. At no time did Schrag argue or offer any resistance. In town the mob ordered Schrag to buy War Bonds; he refused but did offer to contribute two hundred dollars to the Salvation Army or the Red Cross. The mob ordered Schrag to salute the flag and carry it at the head of the parade. Upon his refusal, someone tried to force a flag in his hands and it dropped to the ground, at which point someone accused him stepping on the flag. Members of the mob painted Schrag yellow and took him to the jail when the call went out for a rope to hang him. At that point the head of the local Anti-Horse Thief Association, Tom Roberts, stood between the jail door and the mob brandishing a gun and saying, "If you take this man out of jail, you take him over my dead body." The mob dispersed and Schrag was moved for his protection.[35]

The Anti-Horse Thief Association had established itself not just as a fraternal organization focusing on the detection and apprehension of horse thieves, but also as an organization that never condoned vigilante action. Individual lapses may have occurred in rare occasions among chapters, but the parent organization was always swift to investigate and respond to reported stumbles. Working within the law allowed the A.H.T.A. to continue to grow and prosper.

Chapter 8

Trail of the Anti-Horse Thief Association

The stars over the western prairie seemed to portend the success of the Anti-Horse Thief Association. The western frontier was growing quickly and the A.H.T.A. provided a valuable service to those pioneers. The A.H.T.A. provided an intelligence system that tracked known and potential thieves, a weekly newspaper for disseminating information of mutual interest, a ladies auxiliary, and an organization that was so well trained to respond to horse theft that they could also be called upon to fight other crime. The organization birthed in Missouri to combat horse theft soon became one of the largest and most powerful fraternal organizations the western frontier had ever seen.

The Black Book

One part of the secret work of the A.H.T.A. was the collection and distribution of suspected and known horse thieves and criminals. Not unique to the A.H.T.A., although it was the largest, this early data base would be created for each lodge community and reported to the state chapter, who would in turn compile the data into one "Black Book" that would then be distributed back to each lodge. This data base was often used in the detection of horse thieves when fresh pursuit was not an option. This process was mentioned in 1883 during the Second Annual Kansas Meeting by the grand worthy president:

For rascals know that when the anties, (as our members are often called,) are strong and energetic that escape from them is nearly impossible, because each member serves as a detective; and each sub-order has a list and minute description of all known and suspected rogues within the jurisdiction of the national order; also the name, post office and telegraph station of every worthy president and worthy secretary in the United States, and secret signs by which they can recognize each other when they meet.[1]

The Constitution of the Grand and Subordinate Orders of the A.H.T.A. of Missouri (A complete copy of this constitution can be found in Appendix 3) described it in Article Twelve:

BLACK BOOK.

Sec. 1. It shall be the duty of each Subordinate Order, to keep a black book, for the purpose of recording the names and residences of all suspicious characters, known criminals, expelled members, and rejected candidates, and each Subordinate Order shall furnish a copy of such person or persons to each subordinate Order in that jurisdiction.

Sec. 2. It shall be the duty of the Worthy Secretary to use all due diligence to ascertain the whereabouts of all suspected persons, rejected candidates and expelled member and report same to the G.W.S. of the Grand Order and he to the G.W.S. of the sister States. But list of rejected candidates shall be published.

The "Black Book" proved to be a powerful tool in the pursuit and apprehension of all sorts of criminals— unsurprisingly, many local law enforcement officers/sheriffs were members of the A.H.T.A. This precursor to the National Crime Information Center (NCIC) was a strong incentive to law enforcement officers to join and have access to this tool. The problem inherent in researching secret societies or the secret work of fraternal societies is that often little remains of the secret work. A copy of the 1901 criminal list for Oklahoma (no publisher listed) was sent to the Kansas

Historical Society[2] along with a cover letter stating that it was from the archives of Fairview Lodge No. 35 (Oklahoma). The following are some examples from this document:

> Clarence Hedge, about 5ft 10in., light complexion, horse trader and farmer, supposed to belong to a gang of horse thieves which operates from somewhere east of Guthrie west to the Glass Mountains.
>
> Dr. Stansbury, perjurer and all around fraud. A thief sympathizer, a regular family disturber.
>
> Mint John, height 5 ft 9 in, weight 150, light complexion, sandy mustache, 30 years old-noted for pure cussedness of all kinds.
>
> "Jack" Goodin, 6 ft 2 inches high; aged 40 years, slender build, dark sandy complexion, brown, deep-set eyes, walks erect. Occupation, horse-trader and racer and horse thief. Residence one and one half miles east of Dale.
>
> Dick Meadows, a man about 5 ft 11 in., weighs about 180, light complexion, cross-eyed. Stopping place Cedarvale, Kansas, and Salt Creek, Osage Nation. Horse Thief.
>
> John Thompson; residence 5 miles east and 1/2 mile south of Shanner; 6 feet high, heavy build, weight about 185, stoop-shouldered, dark hair turning grey, dark skinned, aged 28 or 30 years. All-around crook.
>
> Sam Cooper, about 6 ft, weight about 160, light complected. A horse thief.
>
> Mrs. Jemima Goodson, dark complexion; dark hair; dark eyes; about 5 ft high; weighs 120 pounds; harbors horse thieves. Put out of the Osage Nation for the same and is now living in Pawnee.[2]

Each of the many entries were listed by lodge to help narrow down the geography of the suspects listed in the book. Names of persons who had been convicted in the past, were in prison expecting parole, and were just deemed suspicious were included. Concerns that the true thief would use a disguise or move and the possibility of slander kept the black books secret. These concerns also kept a colorful insight to our communities of the past and the A.H.T.A. closed to the present.

As the Anti-Horse Thief Association continued to grow, it formed many partnerships and consolidated with many similar organizations. One of the larger partnerships was with the Central Protective Association (CPA) formed in 1863, the same year the AHTA originated, in the northwest corner of Missouri. Delegates from both national organizations could be found attending, as guests, the other's respective state and national meetings. *The Anti-Horse Thief Weekly News* also became the official newspaper of the CPA and in the January 1, 1903 edition the president of the CPA wrote: "I am glad to announce to members of the CPA . . . that a working agreement has been made with the AHTA . . . seeking prestige for neither order but the interest of both. . . . I am assured that this agreement will be faithfully kept by the members of both orders. . . . I believe we now enter upon the most important era of our history. Our facilities for suppressing outlawing and bringing thieves to justice have been greatly enlarged."[3] The same issue of the newspaper printed a notice, typical of the long tradition already established between the AHTA and the CPA. Written by a member of the CPA in Bendena, Kansas, it warns of a horse thief believed to be operating in a particular area and includes his name, physical description, and ends with "Arrest him and hold him until I come and get $25 reward."[4]

W.W. Graves

If Maj. David McKee gave birth to and raised the Anti-Horse Thief Association it was W.W. Graves who brought it into adulthood. A newsman and printer by trade, Graves became a driving force in the Anti-Horse Thief Association with the publication of the *Anti-Horse Thief Weekly News* (the Oklahoma Indian Territory had a similar newspaper for members of the AHTA called the *Searchlight*). W.W. Graves established the *AHTA Weekly News* in early 1902 as the official publication of the Anti-Horse Thief Association. The paper was published by Graves for thirty years and eventually reached a circulation of 20,000. This newspaper created the opportunity to share information between lodges and state chapters, became a major symbol of legitimacy to the AHTA, and became a great recruiting tool for the association. His editorial policies and position as publisher place Graves as one of the most influential members of the AHTA, a status that he took seriously and that gained him the respect of many.

Graves also used his writing skills outside the *Anti-Horse Thief Weekly News* to further the professionalization of the AHTA. His *Graves' Manual* was published in 1904 and long served as the handbook for parliamentary issues for the AHTA and the Central Protective Association. Thirty-one pages in length, this book offered procedural issues for local, state, and national chapters of the AHTA, adopted and approved by the National Order in 1904.

The following year Graves wrote *Tricks of Rascals,* a book that outlined the tricks and behaviors of horse thieves and con men of the day. Referenced extensively in Chapter Two of this book, *Tricks of Rascals* covered many of the swindles common in rural areas and acted as a consumer alert. "By a careful study of these rascally tricks many an honest man may be put on his guard and thus know how to deal with strangers with oily tongues and plausible stories and save themselves from being caught in some slick game."[5] Once one was armed with the ability to identify the rascal, one needed to know the law and procedural rules in his apprehension. This issue was addressed by Graves in the following year.

In 1906 Graves published *Law for Criminal Catchers.* This tome became something of a Bible for members of the AHTA covering the basic elements of criminal law and procedure with specific statute information for the states of Arkansas, Kansas, and Missouri. Particular attention was paid to the issues of arrest and search and seizure. Specific laws

W.W. Graves. Photograph courtesy of Osage Mission-Neosho County Museum

covered dealt with theft of livestock, general larceny, and business crimes. Any one of these books, or the newspaper, would have been enough to place the individual as a major contributor to the association; Graves did them all and more.

In 1914 Graves wrote *The Anti-Horse Thief Association: It's Origin and Principles,* which the author admits is primarily a collection of articles that appeared in the *Anti-Horse Thief Weekly News*. Its forty-eight pages contain valuable information of the history, purpose, and organizational structure of the AHTA and is always written through a rose-colored lens that reflects the passion and love of the organization held by the author. W.W. Graves was also the author of fifteen other books with topics that included local history, the Osage Indian Nation, and prominent pioneer figures within the Catholic Church.

Graves was a strong supporter of the merging of the various anti-horse stealing societies, or at the least creating a partnership so that all could operate more effectively. This was not a new concept for the AHTA, which was originally created to have each sub-order to operate in a small, geographically defined area. The Washington Township Protective Society in Lee County, Iowa, was created in 1858 and once word had reached them of the creation of the Grand Order of the AHTA, they asked to be incorporated into the larger association.[6] Graves often would travel out of the state of Kansas to meet with other societies, always extolling the virtues of the AHTA and whenever possible encouraging that they consider joining forces with the largest of such organizations. This proved successful in many cases and added to the roles and success of the AHTA. In the case of the Central Protective Association, the CPA, a formal partnership was reached, which included the sharing of intelligence reports and a month page in the *Anti-Horse Thief Weekly News*.

The formal partnership with the CPA took place as the result of a resolution from the October 1, 1902 national

meeting of the AHTA after a campaign and the strong
support of W.W. Graves. The resolution appointed Graves
as a delegate with the instruction to attend the annual
meeting of the CPA held later that month and to present
an offer of a formal partnership. The CPA approved the
concept and called for a conference with representatives
of the CPA, the Kansas and Missouri divisions of the AHTA,
and W.W. Graves representing the National Association.
The following results were reported in the *Anti Horse Thief
Weekly News*:

> The advisability of cooperation was taken for granted and the
> agreement to join hands in the fight against evil doers was
> adopted by common consent without debate. . . . It shall be the
> duty of any sub-order of either association to respond to the
> call of a sub-order of the other association for aid in detecting
> and arresting criminals and recovering stolen property. . . .
> to get up recognition and test signs whereby a member of
> either association may make himself known and prove his
> membership to the members of the other association.[7]

Graves had to have been aware of the American Protective
Association, an anti-Catholic society cloaked in a patriotic
organization that was created in 1887, two decades after the
birth of the Ku Klux Klan and twenty four years after the
birth of the AHTA. Graves never shied away from issues of
faith when writing about the AHTA:

> The Church is recognized as the greatest exponent of good
> in the world. It develops the finer qualities of mankind and
> teaches all that is good, noble and true. Were it not for the
> influence of the church the position of man would not be
> many stages above that of a brute. Look up and life up has
> always been a rule of the church, and all who follow the spirit
> of the teachings of the church are benefited thereby.
>   There are people in this world who will not listen to the
> voice of the church or take heed of its teachings. They may
> believe there is a God but they recognize no religion. The
> large part of these as well as many who hypocritically profess

religion, have no respect for the laws of God or man. For these the A.H.T.A. was instituted.[8]

W.W. Graves had great fidelity to his faith, and on May 31, 1952 he was made a Knight of St. Gregory, conferred by Pope Pius XII in recognition of his literary contributions to the Catholic Church. It was announced by His Excellency, the Most Rev. Mark K. Carroll, bishop of the Diocese of Wichita. This was the highest honor extended to a lay person by the Catholic Church. On the same date, W.W. Graves was made an Honorary Member of the Osage Nation. The Osage Nation, departing from a normal refusal to accept others into the nation, made Graves an honorary chief of the Osages. This honor was conferred by Paul Pitts, chief of the Osages, who spoke briefly of their esteem for Graves. He was presented with a feathered headdress, the token of honorary membership into the tribe. Graves was named Wy-La-Za-Xa-Ne-Ka-Zhin, which is interpreted as "Mr. Man of the Journal." As his influence and activities within the AHTA started to wane, there was a corresponding increase in members of the Ku Klux Klan joining the AHTA and other anti-horse-thief societies. In his preface to *Origins and Principles,* Graves wrote "Much more could be written about the splendid work of this remarkable organization" and the same is true of this remarkable man.

Ladies Auxiliary

Although women could not join (and later attend meetings of) the AHTA, they were afforded its protection through the payment of dues. The first "Ladies' Social and Aid Society" was organized in 1909 by Mrs. Maggie Taylor, in Sedan, Kansas. Taylor became the first president of the auxiliary, which included members throughout Kansas, Illinois, Missouri, and Oklahoma. The Preamble of the 1916 Kansas Constitution provides a glimpse into its purpose:

We, The State Order, including the members of the Subordinate Orders of the Ladies' Auxiliary of the Anti-Horse

Thief Association of Kansas and jurisdiction, in order to aid
the sick and needy and in the promotion of benevolence,
charity, social culture, mental improvement and education,
and in assisting members in distress in any way necessary, do
mutually agree to be governed . . .[9]

The Ladies Auxiliary became the social and benevolent
arm of the AHTA, looking after the sick and needy members
of the association and giving the women, whose husbands and
sons were members, the ability to participate in meaningful
work during local, regional, and national meetings. Started
in Kansas, the history of the Ladies Auxiliary shows women
from Kansas typically held the majority of offices and had
the greatest number of members in the national order. The
Ladies Auxiliary, as a sister organization of the AHTA, was
considered a secret order with secret signs and passwords
not unlike their male counterpart.

By the late 1930s the Ladies Auxiliary had defined its aims
and objectives as: creating better homes with more religious
teachings for the children; helping to procure homes for
the unfortunate; protecting young girls from white-slave
trafficking; teaching boys and girls to avoid drug and liquor
habits; teaching foreigners how to become good American
citizens; aiding the sick and needy, especially children;
doing all within our power to eliminate crime; and assisting
the Anti-Thief Association (AHTA changed their name to
ATA in 1926) in all their work.

Membership was limited to those who had a family
member in the AHTA. If married, her husband must be a
member of the AHTA, or if single or widowed a woman can
become a member if her father, brother, or son is a member.
In 1908 Miss Jessie Johnson of Salina, Kansas, was made
the first woman honorary member of the Kansas Anti-
Horse Thief Association, and she is believed to be the first
woman member nationally. Her membership was bestowed
during the annual AHTA convention held in Salina, Kansas.
Although it was very rare that any woman would be admitted,

honorary or otherwise, to the AHTA, the Leatherwood Anti-Horse Thief Association of Pennsylvania (which was not part of the AHTA) admitted Mrs. John Smith to its membership rolls in 1887 in place of her husband who had died. The Ladies Auxiliary stayed active through the mid 1940s until the demise of the AHTA.

Bank Robberies

The late-nineteenth century saw corporations and business confronted with expectations of a criminal justice system that was incongruent with reality. Both citizens and corporate owners were concerned over crime, yet "the interests of large corporate ranchers, as well as the interests of railroads and banks, in trying to put an end to cattle rustling and robberies, were quite different than the concern of an outraged citizenry over firearms violations or the theft of a horse."[10] As bank robberies continued to increase and threaten the bottom line, and the traditional methods of intervention and prevention proved wanting, the AHTA was called to provide assistance.

The first decade of the nineteenth century saw an increase of bank robberies in Kansas. In December 1910, J.N. Dolley, the Kansas Bank Commissioner, wrote a letter to the president of the Anti-Horse Thief Association in Parsons, Kansas. In his letter he states:

> *The determination of the Kansas State Bankers Association is to use every means and power at their command to stop this nefarious outlawry, and thus protect and guard the property and lives of this splendid class of Kansas Citizenship. The officers of this Association have great confidence in your association and are much interested in the splendid work you have done in the past in upholding our several laws and assisting to insure the safety of our people and the security of their property against loss by thieves, robbers, murders [sic], vagrants, tramps, incendiaries, and all violators of the law and I trust that every state bank in Kansas will petition and be accepted to*

full membership in your association, and assure you that we will do our part in aiding and assisting you in carrying on your splendid work.[11]

When seeking all the resources available to combat crime from the corporate perspective, the Anti-Horse Thief Association was identified as a key ingredient for the recipe of safe and secure banking. In his 1912 Biennial Report, Dolley wrote:

1912— Two of the worst gangs of bank robbers which have ever infested the Middle West were operating in the state of Kansas at the time I took active charge of the banking department. . . . In the years of 1908, 1909, 1910, and the first three months of 1911, there were one hundred twenty-five banks robbed in the states of Oklahoma, Nebraska, Arkansas, Missouri, Texas, and Kansas, thirty-eight of which were in this state. Kansas was apparently helpless to prevent these outrages against it citizens and their properties. In March 1911, this department secured a special appropriation from the legislature and employed one of the best detectives in the United States, Mr. J.S. Searls. We began to make a campaign against the bank robber in Kansas. We worked in conjunction with the Anti-Horse Thief Association, the United States government, and various other officers and organizations.

Both of the gangs mentioned above have been completely wiped out. As a result of this work, not a single bank has been robbed in Kansas since that time, and only one attempt, while the other states mentioned have had as many or more than ever before.[12]

Bank Commissioner Dolley recognized that what the Anti-Horse Thief Association had in place was a statewide network of volunteers trained in the detection and apprehension of criminals. It was not much of a stretch for the AHTA to broaden its scope to include bank robberies. Many of the early anti-horse-thief societies and associations expanded their focus into a broader scope of crimes while several started with that very concept in mind. In the case of: *Marsh v. Wells Fargo Company Express* (88 Kan. 538; 129 P. 168; 1913 Kan.) an express messenger on the Atchison, Topeka & Santa Fe Railway was murdered in Marion County, Kansas, on March 29, 1908. Special agents of the express company and law enforcement decided that the prudent course of action must include notifying members of the Anti-Horse Thief Association, which was done. Although members did not capture the suspect, later convicted, it is worth notice that the AHTA was deemed as an important step in tracking down a murderer.

Equine Precedents

The work of the Anti-Horse Thief Association often resulted in the capture/arrest of criminals and thus did not escape the scrutiny of the courts. As noted earlier in this chapter often the AHTA would track down, apprehend, and usually assist in the prosecution. Legal conflicts and questions were inevitable as the following cases demonstrate.

In the Oklahoma case of *J.P. Crawford v. George W. Ferguson*, County Judge Crawford was charged with a violation of prohibitory liquor law and asked the Court of Criminal Appeals to replace Judge Ferguson in the case, because Ferguson was a member of the AHTA and as a member had helped police in bootlegging enforcement, not related to the case in hand. They did not replace the judge and in the opinion the court wrote:

> One of the most useful organizations in the state is the Anti-Horse-Thief Association. The people have just as much right to organize to assist the officers to enforce the law against the bootlegger as they have to organize to assist the officers to enforce the law against the horse thief. Of the two, the horse thief is the least dangerous to the lives and character of the people, and the peace and good order of society. Who would say that, because a juror or judge may belong to or

be in sympathy with the Anti-Horse-Thief Association, he would thereby be disqualified from taking part in the trial of a defendant charged with theft? The writer of this opinion was for years attorney for the Anti-Horse-Thief Association. He confesses to a strong prejudice against horse stealing, but he has no prejudice against any individual, simply because he may be charged with this offense, until such person has been proven to be guilty by competent evidence beyond a reasonable doubt. On account of the infamous character of the crime, he would require conclusive proof of the guilt of a defendant before believing him to be guilty.[13]

In the *State of Iowa v. C.J. Van Hoozer* case, the defendant was convicted for the theft of a car. In his appeal, he argued that a juror was a member of the Anti-Horse Theft Association and was allowed to sit over his objections. He stated that the AHTA was formed for the expressed purpose to "bring to justice persons who may be guilty of stealing horses or automobiles, and that the juror had contributed to a fund which is used by said association to give rewards to persons who secure the conviction of those who steal automobiles within a certain territory."[14] The juror stated that his membership in the AHTA would not bias his judgment and the court did not see this as an error.

The "Sanctity of Womanhood" is a term that appears many times in AHTA literature, and its meaning is demonstrated in the following two cases. In the Missouri case *State v. Wilkins Taylor*, the defendant was found guilty of rape. In his appeal, he objected that members of the AHTA carried out a public relations campaign to support the prosecutor and to intimidate the attorneys and witnesses of the defense. Large numbers of members attended the trial and defense council made several objections to "voices in audience" that make remarks, clap hands, or laugh after statements that seemed to injure the defense and support the prosecution.[15]

In *State of Kansas v. Maurice E. Waterman*, the defendant was convicted of obtaining illicit connection, under a promise of marriage. The defendant fled to the state of Oklahoma and it took some time before he was arrested. "When defendant was brought back from Oklahoma he was met by numerous neighbors and acquaintances, gathered under the auspices of the Anti-Horse Thief Association, and upon their suggestion he consented to marry the prosecuting witness, and the ceremony took place before a justice of the peace, when he immediately deserted his wife."[16] It seems that the quick work and rapid response of riders did not have a lasting impact on thieves of the heart.

IT WAS BRED IN OLD MISSOURI
Joplin (Mo.) News Herald

Kansas, Missouri, and Illinois owe much to the efficiency of the Anti-Horse Thief Association, its efforts have accomplished what the officers of the law have failed to bring about. Law-breakers have learned to fear this organization of public-spirited citizens so that the object of the association, protection as well as detection are secured with a minimum of exertion.

Clark County, Missouri claims the credit for establishing this order. Major David McKee and a few others formed the first organization in 1863, and at the present time about 35,000 people are enrolled under its banner. Since the history of prosecutions through the central Mississippi valley has proved the good purposes of the organization.

In accordance with a recent request of the president of the association, ministers in every community have been asked to speak tomorrow on "Public Morals and Respect for the Law." The recent increase in crime in various sections of the country has made this request seem advisable to the organization, and it is hoped that the request will be generally observed.

Public sentiment should be responsive to this plea. Unless public sentiment does crystallize in favor of better observations and stricter enforcement of the law the outcome of tax methods can be for-seen without much trouble. If the Anti-Horse Thief Association can foster a better spirit toward the law, its existence will not only be justified again, but unusual praise will be due the organization.

—*A.H.T.A. Weekly News*, January 30, 1908

Klan and Horse Thief Detectives

Gresham attributes the greatest decline of members in the AHTA to the Ku Klux Klan. In the 1920s, "thousands of Antis became Klansmen and in many communities, anti orders ceased to function because their members became Klansmen."[17] Because both were operating as secret societies, it is difficult to document the infiltration of the Klan into the A.H.T.A. but they gained more of a stronghold as W.W. Graves, a staunch Catholic and supporter of the national and Kansas chapter, started to gradually be less involved. Not unique to the AHTA, the Klan targeted the various anti-horse-thief societies because they had proven organizational structures, had built-in intelligence groups, had established communication systems, operated in secret, and in many states had the power of arrest.

In 1843, Illinois College located in Jacksonville, Illinois was known to be part of the Underground Railroad with faculty, staff, and students being conductors. In one case a woman from Louisiana came to Jacksonville with her child and a slave who was the nurse for the child. Because Illinois was a free state, the nurse could claim her freedom—a fact that she learned from a student of the college, as he took her

to the father of a college mate who agreed to act as conductor. A confrontation occurred before they could leave, legal action was taken, and the public became outraged. A town meeting was held at the courthouse on February 23, 1843 where many people voiced concern that the general public might assume the whole town endorsed the actions of the college abolitionists. Four resolutions were presented (the resolutions were printed in newspapers in the contiguous states and throughout the South) including:

> *Resolved,* That the citizens of Jacksonville will at all times extend the hand of friendship and hospitality to their acquaintances in the South, and will be pleased to reciprocate the friendly relations of neighbors, ready at all times and on all occasions, promptly and efficiently to aid and protect them in the enjoyment of their property. And to that end, having reasons to believe that there are regular bands of abolitionists, organized with depots and relays of horses to run negroes through our State to Canada, and that one of them is in this town, we will form an Anti-Negro Stealing Society, as we heretofore formed an Anti-Horse Stealing Society, and that we will, in this neighborhood, break up the one as we broke up the other.[18]

The organizational structure and effectiveness of the earlier Anti-Horse Stealing Society was used as an example to encourage the creation of a "Pre-Klan" society. The value of the infrastructure of anti-horse thief societies was recognized by racists almost a quarter century before the creation of the Invisible Empire. Sixty years after it was established, the Ku Klux Klan was looking to expand its membership and once again turned to anti-horse thief societies. This time the Klan focused on Indiana and Ohio.

The Thief Detecting Company for the Detection and Apprehension of Horse Thieves and Others Charged with Crime, has a transcript of an act to incorporate the company in the Indiana legislature approved January 21, 1850. Section six of the act states:

The members of the corporation while engaged in the
service of pursuing or arresting offenders within the State,
shall have all the power of Sheriffs and constables in calling to
their assistance the power of the county, and for a refusal to
assist or obey the call of such members the person so refusing
shall be subject to the same penalties as upon a refusal to
obey the Sheriff of the county.[19]

The act gave the anti-horse thief association the power
of arrest, which was extended when the Indiana legislature
sanctioned by statute the organization of men in various
counties for the purpose of arresting horse thieves and other
felons. A few citizens could group themselves together, apply
for a certificate to the Secretary of State, have this certificate
approved by the three commissioners of the county in which
these sleuths were to function, and then they were officially
recognized. At once they obtained the powers of a constable,
and, unlike the average policeman, they were under no bond
for the correct and faithful performance of their duties. "The
early development of the Invisible Empire in Indianapolis
and the state was largely made under the auspices of the
Horse Thief Detective Association."[20] Under Klan control,
the HTDA functioned as a vigilante unit, "stopping and
searching automobiles on the highways, raiding vice dens,
driving through the Negro district in Indianapolis with guns
drawn, and the protecting the privacy of Klan meetings."[21]
At that time the majority of the anti-horse thief societies
in Indiana were organized under the National Horse Thief
Detective Association when Klansman David Clarke
Stephenson entered the state organization and saw them
as the enforcement arm which gave him the opportunity of
". . . organizing his own police force and proclaiming, 'I am
the law.'"[22]

David Clarke Stephenson (known as the "old man" even
though he was in his thirties) quickly became the political
boss of Republican politics in the state of Indiana. From
local offices to the governor, one did not plan on running

on the Republican ticket without first gaining the blessing of Stephenson—a blessing that came with a cost. So powerful was his influence that "One newspaper described the 1924 Republican state convention as a Klan Kloncilium, with Stephenson's choices for major officers—from local school boards up to governor—winning, along with the Hooded Order's favored presidential candidate, Calvin Coolidge. Most had promised their allegiance to 'The Old Man' in return for his support, some even agreeing to consult with him on appointments."[23]

Stephenson was known to live life large and fast, which ended up bringing about his downfall. He had taken up with one Madge Oberholtzer, a single twenty-eight-year-old statehouse employee. In March of 1925 Oberholtzer went to Stephenson's home, where the two drank heavily. Later that evening, he forced her aboard his private drawing room on a train bound for Chicago and en route attacked her, badly "chewing" her body. The next day Oberholtzer, despondent, left Stephenson and consumed some poison. "In spite of her pain, she repeatedly refused Stephenson's offer to take her to a hospital if she would marry him. She died several weeks later, and Stephenson was charged with her murder. The well-publicized trial ended in a conviction of second-degree murder and a life sentence, and the downfall of the Indiana Klan and its hand-picked politicians."[24] Stephenson banked on all the political favors owed to him to avoid punishment, but when there was no favorable appeal or pardon by the summer of 1927 he released to the public his records of all the "deals" struck and favors granted for contributions. His revelations resulted in a firestorm of bribery and graft trials that reached from local offices straight through to Gov. Ed Jackson.

The Klan's influence was not unique to Indiana; it was also felt in Ohio and Kansas. In Youngstown, Ohio, 1922 "the mantle of leadership fell to Colonel E.A. Gunder, who had directed the Klan's Horse Thief Detective Association (similar to that of Indiana)."[25] In Kansas the Klan had long participated in parades of such organizations as the Central Protective Association, an anti-horse thief society located throughout the northeastern part of the state. In the mid-1920s the Klan membership approached 40,000 which "so alarmed William Allen White that the famed *Emporia* editor entered the 1924 gubernatorial campaign solely to dramatize the extent of the hooded influence in Kansas."[26] Many in Kansas left the AHTA to join the Klan and when the Stephenson scandal broke in Indiana, membership in the AHTA continued to drop. The scar left by the Klan involvement festered and became one of the causes of the death of the AHTA.

Happy Trails

World War I, the involvement and infiltration by the Klan, the Great Depression, the Dust Bowl, and the rise of the automobile as the primary means of transportation all led to a steady decline in the membership of the AHTA. Minutes from annual meetings of the national and state chapters show that the officers and general membership struggled to maintain relevance in a rapidly changing world. After many years of debate, in 1926 the Anti-Horse Thief Association changed their name to the Anti-Theft Association (ATA). It was during the late 1920s that many lodges closed shop, finding that the telephone replaced relay stations, the automobile replaced the horse, and law enforcement increased in effectiveness and efficiency in urban communities to the point that the ATA slowed rather than enhanced response time.

In 1926 the organization adopted the name Anti-Theft Association to more accurately reflect its changing operational function. "The automobile was then fast becoming a factor in our national life and many believed that a change of the name would draw men to the Anti fold."[27] This idea was not really one made in haste. In 1883 the

Kansas president stated in his annual address ". . . the Anti-Horse Thief Association (which should more appropriately be called 'The Anti-Crime Association,') from its birth to the present time."[28] Preventing automobile theft quickly took over as the primary purpose of the AHTA/ATA as the following Kansas State Chapter records indicate:

Kansas A.H.T.A.	1917	1920	1922	1930	1931	1932
Horses Stolen	11	5	1	2	1	2
Recovered	9	10	0	1	0	1
Automobiles Stolen	46	37	29	9	9	7
Recovered	40	29	21	8	12	5
Thieves Caught	73	90	51	85	48	18
Convicted	60	69	35	73	15	28

The automobile was only one of many factors that resulted in the decline and eventual death of the AHTA. Even though the automobile replaced the horse and the states saw the creation of more effective law enforcement agencies, communication issues still kept the ATA in play as an active force in the detection and apprehension of criminals. As telephone service entered the western states, it was not uncommon for rural communities to have telephone service only during business hours and the early evening. When the switchboard was not staffed, law enforcement could not be called. "At present, in the nighttime, the telephone systems in most of the smaller towns are closed down for the night. The auto thief knows this, and generally avoids the larger towns with his stolen cars."[29] The AHTA system of communication and pursuit, which was modified for the telephone and automobile, led many members of law enforcement to join the local lodges. More than just a community or fraternal activity, the AHTA had an established intelligence-reporting system, a communication system allowing contact across state lines, and members willing to be trained and assist law enforcement in the pursuit and apprehension of criminals. By 1940 the *Anti-Theft News* started running the banner "The only Publication in the United States Devoted to Rural Crime Prevention News," indicating the organization's shift to maintain relevance in the changing country. Rural Arkansas, Illinois, Kansas, Missouri and Oklahoma still had small law enforcement agencies, telephone systems that did not operate twenty-four hours a day, and a real need for some form of auxiliary police, but change was in the air, even for them. In the October 1940 edition of the *ATA News* an article titled "Danger Ahead" focused not on the pending war in Europe but the end of the association.

> Following the World War the A.H.T.A. Order suffered heavy with-drawls of local orders and members. . . . the real issue was that the Order was not flexible enough to meet quickly a situation brot [brought] about by the rapid change of thought. This led to a discussion of dropping the "Horse" from the name of the Order and this was finally done in 1926. This caused still further withdrawls from the Order. The mere changing of the Automobile and later of modern police methods in dealing with crime-the Order needed a new program.[30]

As the struggle for relevance continued, specialized groups, such as the Anti-Automobile Thief Association of America or the Anti-Dog Theft Association, took additional members and interest from the ATA. Members started turning attention to "Anti-American Activities" and as the United States entered the Second World War, the ATA and the rest of the country on the home front focused on supporting the war and American troops. Soldiers returning home found a country transformed, a country technologically advanced by the war effort, a country building suburbs and highways, and a country that no longer had need for an Anti-Horse Thief Association.

The two World Wars saw a decline in membership as the

younger members joined the service and the older members devoted their lives to supporting the war effort on the home front. Between the wars, the economic depression and the rise of the Ku Klux Klan and their infiltration into the various anti-horse thief societies served as yet another major blow to the membership. The end of World War II saw the conversion of the war machine into civilian production resulting in advances in automobiles, communication systems, and improvements in law enforcement. As the nation turned its focus from depression and war to the future, very few took notice of the Anti-Horse Thief Association as it rode off into the sunset.

Appendix 1

Anti-Horse Thief Societies[1]

Name of Society	State	Year of Origin
Independent Order of the Knights of the Horse	AR	1884
Woodstock Theft Detection Society	CT	1793
Glastonbury Association for the Detecting Horse Thieves	CT	1796
Kent Association for Detecting Horse Thieves	CT	1801
The Enfield Society for the Detection of Thieves and Robbers	CT	1823
New Milford Horse Thief and Burglar Detective Association	CT	1873
Redding Anti-Horse Thief Association	CT	1885
Danbury Anti-Horse Thief Association	CT	1896
Friends of Justice	DE	1786
Anti Horse Thief Association of Winchester	IA	1839
Muscatine County Horse-Thief Association	IA	1857
Mitchell County Protective Association Against Horse Thieves	IA	1873
Protective Association of Pottawatamie County	IA	Unknown
Greenview Rangers	IL	1859
Eliza Association for the Detection of Thieves	IL	1864
Randolph Horse Thief Detecting Society	IL	1865
Scottville Horse Thief Detecting Society AKA: Mt. Zion Self-Protective Society	IL	1883
Alhambra Anti-Thief Association	IL	1927
Arenzville Anti-Horse Thief Association	IL	Unknown
Eagle Creek Marion Co. Horse Thief Detecting Company	IN	1850
Newton and Spring Valley Horse Thief Detecting Company	IN	1854
Cain Township Horse Thief Detective Company	IN	1884

Guilford Detective Association	IN	1897
Seward Detective Company	IN	1898
Lexington Horse Thief Association	IN	1902
Wabash General Association of Horse Thief Detective Companies[2]	IN	1860
Wild Cat Horse Guards	KS	1877
Kansas Valley Detective Association	KS	1879
Atchison County Protective Association	KS	1889
Whitewater Anti-Horse Thief Association	KS	1900
Northampton Society for the Detection of Thieves and Robbers	MA	1782
Oxford Society for the Detection of Horsestealers and Thieves	MA	1791
Massachusetts Society for Detecting Horse Thieves	MA	1795
Society for Detecting Horse Thieves in the Towns of Mendon, Bellingham, and Milford	MA	1795
Rehoboth, Seekonk and Pawtucket Detecting Society	MA	1796
Norton Detecting Society Formed for the Purpose of Detecting Horse Thieves and Recovering Horses	MA	1797
Norfolk, and Bristol [Counties] Horse Thief Detecting Society	MA	1802
Society in Dedham for Apprehending Horse Thieves	MA	1816
Society in Roxbury, Brookline, and Brighton for Apprehending Horse Thieves	MA	1819
Newton, Needham and Natick Society for Apprehending Horse Thieves	MA	1822
Sheffield Association for the Detection of Horse Thieves	MA	1869
Rising Sun Detective Association	MD	1880
Niles Horse Thief Association	MI	1853
Cooper Vigilance Society	MI	1879
Lakeside Horse Thief Association	MI	Unknown
St. Joseph County Mutual Protection Association	MI	Unknown
Anti-Cattle and Horse Thief Society of Freeborn County	MN	1862
Waseca County Horse Thief Detectives	MN	1864
Central Protection Association	MO	1870
Southwest Missouri Protective Association	MO	1886
Elm Grove Horse Detective Society	MO	1914
Madison County Horse Thief Dectective Association	MO	1914
Anti-Horse Thief Society of Buffalo County	NE	1879
Walpole Society for Bringing to Justice Horse Thieves and Pilferers	NH	1816

Keene Horse Thief Detecting Society	NH	Unknown
Ackquackanonk Township	NJ	1787
Paramus Society for the Detection of Horse Thieves	NJ	1818
Alexandria Vigilant Society for Detecting Horse Thieves and Mutually Insuring Horses Stolen	NJ	1818
Washington Association for the Apprehension of Horse Thieves	NJ	1820
So. Jersey Pursing and Detecting Society	NJ	1824
Burlington & Gloucester Co's Assn. for Detection of Horse Thieves	NJ	1828
Kingwood Vigilance Society	NJ	1835
Union Society for the Detection of Horse Thieves	NJ	1839
Mercer County Pursuing and Detecting Society	NJ	1843
Burlington & Monmouth Co's Pursing and Detecting Society	NJ	1845
Mt. Laurel Pursuing and Detecting Society	NJ	1870
Moorestown Pursuing and Detecting Society	NJ	Unknown
Mount Hope Vigilant Society for the Detection of Horse Thieves	NY	1817
Schoharie Union Anti-Horse Thief Society	NY	1866
Brunswick Society for Apprehending Horse Thieves	NY	1867
Anti-Horse Thief Society (Rural Grove/Montgomery County)	NY	1870
Anti-Horse Thief Society	NY	1870
Stuyvesant, Kinderhook, and Chatham Detection Society of Horse Thieves	NY	Unknown
The Sherburne Horse-Thief Detective Society	NY	Unknown
Sandlake Association for Mutual Protection Against Horse Thieves	NY	Unknown
Bentonville Anti-Horse Thief Society	OH	1853
Anti-Horse Thief Association – Indian territory Division	OK	Unknown
The Newtown Reliance Company for the Detecting and Apprehending of Horse Thieves and Other Villains	PA	1819
The Fellowship Horse Company	PA	1821
Warren Company for the Recovery of Stolen Horses and Other Property and the Detection of Thieves	PA	1824
Union Association of Newtown and parts adjacent in Delaware County, for detecting horse thieves	PA	1834
Brush Valley Association for the Detection and Apprehension of Horse Thieves	PA	1853
Curllsvile Anti-Horse Thief Company	PA	1856
Leatherwood Anti-Horse Thief Association	PA	1868
Spring Valley Police Company of Crawford County	PA	1869

Salem Anti-Horse Thief Society	PA	1871
East Whiteland Horse Company for the Detection of Horse Thieves	PA	Unknown
Mt. Top Horse Thief Detecting Society	PA	Unknown
York County Horse Thief Detecting Society	PA	Unknown
Willistown Union Association for the Detection of Horse Thieves and Recovery of Stolen Property	PA	Unknown
Coventry Horse Company	PA	Unknown
Pleasantville Horse Company	PA	Unknown
Centre-Square Association of Montgomery County, for the Recovery of Stolen Horses, and Detection of Thieves	PA	Unknown
Skippack Society for the Detection of Horse Thieves	PA	Unknown
Smithfield Society for Detecting Thieves	RI	1793
Cumberland Detective Society	RI	1894
Mt. Meridian League to prevent and punish horse stealing	VA	1867
Mutual Protection Association	VA	1867
Pownal Association to Counteract and Detect Horse Thievery	VT	1789
Shoreham Society for the Apprehension of Horse Thieves	VT	1822
Bennington Association for the Detecting of Horse Thieves	VT	1823
Battenkill Valley Society for Apprehending Horse Thieves	VT	1894
Sprague Stock Protective Association	WA	Unknown
Nepeuskun Anti-Horse Thieves Association	WI	1859
Waukesha County Detective Society	WI	1885
Primrose Anti Horse Thief Association	WI	1891

Multi-State Anti-Horse Thief Societies

Anti-Horse Thief Association AKA / Anti Theft Association	1863
Central Protection Association	1863
Consolidated Vigilant Society of New Jersey and Pennsylvania	1891
National Horse Thief Detective Association	1860
United Horse Companies of Pennsylvania, New Jersey and Delaware	1822

Constitutions

This section contains in its entirety the Constitution of the Center-Square Association of Montgomery County, for the Recovery of Stolen Horses, and Detection of Thieves (1821) and the Constitution of the Scottsville Horse Thief Detecting Society (1883).

CONSTITUTION OF THE CENTER-SQUARE ASSOCIATION OF MONTGOMERY COUNTY, FOR THE RECOVERY OF STOLEN HORSES, AND DETECTION OF THIEVES.

Norristown:
PRINTED BY JAMES WINNARD.
1821.

CONSTITUTION

Article 1. All those who now are, or hereafter may become members of this association, shall have their names entered in a book kept by the secretary, in which the proceedings of the association and this constitution shall be recorded.

Art. 2. A general meeting of the members of the association shall be held annually, on the last Seventh-day in January in every year, in the townships of Whitpain and Gwynedd alternately, at such suitable place as shall have been agreed on by a majority of the members present at the preceding annual meeting-and then and there between the hours of 2 and 6 in the afternoon, elect by ballot, one president, a secretary & treasurer, and four persons as a committee of accounts, who, together, shall be a board of officers for the performance of such duties as are hereinafter assigned them, and shall serve till the next annual meeting, and till others are appointed, and if by death, resignation, removal, or any other disability, any officer elected as aforesaid, be rendered incapable of acting in his office, the board of officers, or a majority of them, shall appoint a suitable person to supply such vacancy till the next annual election. The President shall preside in the meetings of the association, and call occasional meetings when required by the board of officers, or a majority of them.

Art. 3. The secretary shall record the transactions of the association, and give public notice of the time and place of the annual meeting, in such manner as the association may direct.

Art. 4. The treasurer shall receive and pay the money of the association. Before entering on the duties of his office he shall give his bond, in such sum as shall be deemed sufficient, to such persons as the association shall direct, in trust, however, for the use of the association; conditioned for the faithful discharge of his office, and especially that he will, from time to time, pay the money of the association, committed to him by the chairman of the committee of accounts, and deliver the balance that shall be in his hands to his successor in office; rendering, annually, a statement of his accounts.

Art. 5. The committee of accounts shall have the charge and oversight of the funds of the association, and shall meet on notice given by the president, who shall be their chairman, in order to settle the accounts of the association, and levy such sums equally upon the members as they shall find necessary to defray any common expense. A duplicate of the sums laid out at any time shall be delivered to the treasurer, who, within fifteen days after the receipt thereof, shall give notice to each member of the sum he is to pay, and in case any member refuses or fails to pay the same within thirty days after such notice, he shall be expelled the association [*sic*].

Art. 6. The board of officers before mentioned, or a majority of them, shall have the power to call out all or any part of the members of the association, as occasion may require, to pursue any stolen horse or thief, upon information being given them sufficient to warrant such call, and the person so called, immediately, either in person or by a proper substitute, shall be obliged to go in pursuit at least forty-five miles, except those persons whose duty it shall be to examine the city of Philadelphia, and if any member or members shall have good reason to believe that he or they are on the route taken by the object pursued, then he or they shall continue the pursuit as long as they may have a prospect of success, and in case any member shall fail to go in pursuit as aforesaid, he shall forfeit and pay the treasurer, for the use of the association, the sum of *five dollars*. All pleas or excuses for not pursuing as aforesaid shall be determined by a majority of the board officers; but if the person shall think himself aggrieved by their decision, he shall have a right to appeal to the next meeting of the association. If any extraordinary expense shall be incurred in the pursuit, it may be submitted to the board of officers, and if judged reasonable, shall be paid out of the funds of the association.

Art. 7. Every person shall be paid at the common expense, *four cents* per mile for his travel in pursuit and returning he shall likewise receive twenty dollars for arresting the thief and recovering the horse, provided the thief is prosecuted to conviction, or ten dollars for either horse or thief, if the horse had really been stolen, to be paid by the association.

Art. 8. Every member shall within fifteen days after he shall have become the owner of any horse over three years of age, record his age, colour, height and particular marks; and every member neglecting to make and keep such record, shall, if such horse be stolen, pay a fine of ten dollars to the treasurer, at or before the next annual meeting, for the use of the association.

Art. 9. Any member having a horse stolen, shall give immediate information thereof to the board of officers with a record as above directed, (who shall proceed as directed in article sixth) and if such horse shall not be recovered within three months, the owner shall receive from the treasurer the amount of two-thirds of such sum, as any three disinterested persons (to be chosen by ballot by a majority of the association) shall adjudge to have been the value of said horse: But the sum to be actually paid for any stolen horse shall not exceed 100 dollars. If the horse shall be recovered at any time thereafter, it shall be optional with the owner to receive the horse again, upon re-funding the money to the association which he had received, otherwise the horse to be the property of the association.

Art. 10. No person shall be a member who shall not reside within seven miles of the point, where the Swedes ford road crosses the line dividing the townships of Gwynedd and Whitpain, but any member removing out of said limits, shall have liberty to transfer his right of membership to any person within those limits, provided such person shall be approved of by a majority of at least two thirds of the members convened at the next annual meeting.

Art. 11. Candidates for membership shall be nominated by one of the members at an annual meeting, who shall inform the association of the character of the applicant—a vote shall then be taken by ballot, and the consent of two-thirds of the members present shall entitle such applicant to a right of membership, on signing the constitution, and paying such entrance money as the association shall, from time to time, direct.

Art. 12. The members, their executors and administrators, shall have a right to transfer their share or rights in this association to any person who may be approved of by a majority of at least two-thirds of the members convened at an annual meeting.

Art. 13. The sons of respectable citizens, who reside with their fathers, being admitted as members, shall entitle their father's property to the protection of the association in the same manner as if the father himself were a member.

Art. 14. Any number of members, not less than twelve, who shall attend any regularly constituted meeting of the association, shall be a quorum, and competent to the dispatch of business, but a smaller number may appoint the time and place of holding the next meeting, and direct the secretary to advertise accordingly.

Art. 15. Any person may be expelled from this association by two-thirds of the members convened, who may, in their opinion, have conducted himself in an improper manner.

Art. 16. A majority of the members shall have power to pass by-laws, not repugnant to this constitution, and to decide all questions touching the interest of the association not herein otherwise directed, but nothing shall be done either to amend or render void any article of this constitution without the concurrence of two-thirds of the members convened at an annual meeting.

The following resolution was adopted as a plan most proper to pursue for promptly calling out the company in cases of alarm:

Resolved. That when any member shall have good reason to believe that his horse has been stolen, he shall proceed immediately to alarm the board of officers, and also the other members of the association, whose duty it shall be to assist to the upmost of their power in spreading such alarm, and also as soon as possible (consistent with such duty) to repair to the place of rendezvous in order to pursue, if the board of officers should judge it necessary, and any member neglecting to repair to the rendezvous on such call, shall be subject to the same fine as if called by the board of officers; but, if the member whose horse is stolen shall have strong reason to think that he knows the route taken by the thief, he may request two members, living contiguous to him, to pursue on such route, and if such members consent to pursue, they shall be entitled to the same compensation as if required by the board of officers, but no person shall be compelled to pursue on such a call. Place of rendezvous at the house of *Abraham Wentz.*

CONSTITUTION AND BY-LAWS[1]
-OF THE-
SCOTTVILLE
HORSE THIEF
Detecting Society
Scottville, Illinois.
1883

PREAMBLE.

We whose names are here annexed, desirous of forming a society to protect each one of us from the evils and losses attendant upon Horse Stealing and other Robbery, do pledge ourselves to be governed by the following Constitution and By-Laws:

CONSTITUTION.

ARTCLE I.
This Society shall be known as the Mt. Zion Self Protective Society.

ARTCLE II.
The officers of this Society shall consist of a President, Vice-President, Secretary and Treasurer, all to be elected annually by ballot.

ARTICLE III.
It shall be the duty of the President to preside at all the meetings; to enforce a due obedience to the Constitution and By-Laws; to keep a list of all its members and appoint all committees.

Section 1. It shall be the duty of the Vice President to act in the absence of the President.

Section 2. It shall be the duty of the Secretary to keep correct minutes of the proceedings of this Society.

Section 3. It shall be the duty of the Treasurer to keep a correct account of all moneys received; pay all orders drawn on him by the President and report, when called upon, the condition of the Society.

ARTICLE IV.
Any person to become a member of this Society, shall receive a clear ballot and pay a sum of fifty cents.

ARTICLE V.
The regular Quarterly Meetings shall be held on the third Saturday of January, April, July and October.

ARTICLE VI.

The officers shall not be exempt from duty as pursuers.

ARTICLE VII.

There shall be twelve persons appointed quarterly, as their names stand on the list who shall go in pursuit of the thief or furnish a substitute, or on refusal to go or furnish a substitute, shall be fined, not to exceed Five Dollars: — Provided, always, that a reasonable excuse shall be accepted, and the excuse must be made at the first regular meeting.

ARTICLE VIII.

The pursuers shall ride two days, and if they hear any intelligence of the thief they shall pursue as far as they think advisable.

ARTICLE IX.

Any member failing to comply with the requirements herein contained, shall be liable to expulsion.

ARTICLE X.

If any reward be offered for stolen property by parties outside of this Association and the pursuers appointed by the President of the Society shall find the same and receive the reward it shall be the property of the Society.

ARTICLE XI.

No part of this Constitution shall be altered, amended or annulled, except at a regular Quarterly meeting and by a two-thirds vote of the members present, notice being given at the previous meeting.

ARTICLE XII.

The Society shall sit with closed doors and admit no one but members.

We, the Committee on By-Laws, have examined and accepted the By-Laws herein adopted. And add that no member of this Society shall go on a bond of any known thief; and further recommend that any person who may be found guilty of committing an outrage upon any woman shall be dealt with to the fullest extent of the law.

W.C. Drake, J.W. Eades, and E. Brown, Committee.

Appendix 3

A.H.T.A. & Ladies Auxiliary Constitutions

This section contains the 1887 Constitution of the Anti-Horse Thief Association & 1909 Constitution of the Ladies' Social and Aid Society of the AHTA in their entirety with original spellings and errors intact.

CONSTITUTION OF THE
GRAND and SUBORDINATE ORDERS
OF THE **A.H.T.A.**
OF MISSOURI REVISED 1887

HERALD PRINT, PALMYRA, MO.

CONSTITUTION OF THE
GRAND-ORDER OF THE
ANTI-HORSE THIEF ASSOCIATION

ARTICLE I.

NAME AND JURISDICTION.

Section 1. This body shall be known as the Grand Order of the Anti-Horse Thief Association for the State of Missouri and its jurisdiction.

It shall be composed of representatives from Subordinate Orders, and the P.G.W.P.'s and W.P.'s of Subordinate Orders shall be members by virtue of their office, when present.

Sec. 2. This Grand Order shall have jurisdiction over all localities in which there are at present, or may be hereafter, Orders located. It is the supreme tribunal of the Order in the State, and without its sanction no Subordinate Order can exist. It possesses the sole right and power, in the manner hereinafter provided, of granting or suspending charters, of receiving appeals and redressing grievances arising in Orders, of originating and regulating the means of its own support, of deciding all questions arising out of this Constitution or Rules or Order, and of doing all other acts necessary to promote the interest of the Order, provided the same are not in violation of the laws of the land, or consent of the N.O.

ARTICLE II.

OF SESSIONS AND LOCATION.

Sec. 1. The Grand Order shall hold a regular annual session, commencing on the third Wednesday in October of each year, at 10 o'clock, A.M.

Sec. 2. A majority of the representatives of the Subordinate Orders present shall constitute a quorum for the transaction of business.

Sec. 3. The Grand Order shall, during the session, determine by ballot the place of its next annual session, and a majority of all the votes cast shall be necessary to a choice.

Sec. 4. Each Subordinate Order shall be entitled to one representative for the first twelve members, and one additional representative for each additional fifteen members.

Sec. 5. One delegate may cast the entire vote of his Order in the Grand Order.

Sec. 6. Any delegate may represent other Subordinate Orders than his own, in all cases as a regular delegate, provided he bear duly authenticated credentials from such subordinate Orders as he may be called on to represent, but he shall be allowed to cast only one vote for each Subordinate Order except his own, that he may represent.

Sec. 7. No Grand officer or his deputy shall represent in the Grand Order any Sub-order than his own.

ARTICLE III.

OFFICERS AND ELECTIONS.

Sec. 1. The elective officers of the Grand Order shall be Grand Worthy President, Grand Worthy Vice President, Grand Worthy Secretary, Grand Worthy Treasurer, and Grand Worthy Marshall.

Sec. 2. The officers shall be elected at the annual session of the Grand Order, and hold their offices for one year, or until others are elected and installed in their stead.

ARTICLE IV.

DUTIES OF OFFICERS.

Sec. 1. The G.W.P. shall preside at all sessions of the Grand Order, preserve order there in and enforce a due observance of the Constitution of this Grand Order. All questions of order and all decisions made by him shall be subject to an appeal from his decision to the Order, and it shall be his duty to put the question on all such appeals to the Order. He may appoint all officers pro tem., and committees not otherwise provided for. He shall give the casting vote in all cases of tie, except at the election of officers. He shall decide all questions of law which may be made to him from the decision of a W.P. of a subordinate Order. He shall call meetings of the order when business requires it.

Sec. 2. The G.W.V.P. shall act in the absence of the G.W.P., and in the absence of both, the Grand Order shall elect a G.W.P. pro tem.

Sec. 3. The G.W.S. shall make and keep a true record of the proceedings of the Order at every Session, and Transmit immediately after the annual session to the Subordinate Orders copies thereof, receive all moneys, keep a just and correct account of the same, pay them over to the G.W.T. and take his receipt thereof.

He shall issue all necessary notices to subordinates and representatives, and perform such other duties as herein provided for or may be ordered by the Grand Order, and he shall conduct the correspondence of the Order.

Sec. 4. The G.W.T. shall receive all moneys from the hands of the G.W.S., give his receipt for the same, and pay them out only on the warrant of the G.W.P., countersigned by the G.W.S. He shall make a correct report of every annual meeting of the Grand Order of the amount of money in the treasury, and the amount expended since the last report. He shall give bond and security in the sum of one thousand dollars, to be approved by the G.W.P., or the Grand Order, for the faithful performance of his duty.

Sec. 5. The G.W.M. shall be present at all sessions. He shall carry orders from the G.W.P. and G.W.S., and perform all business pertaining to his office; and he shall have power to appoint one or more deputies, as his duties may require.

ARTICLE V.

OFFENCES.

Sec. 1. [Any)] Grand officer may be removed from his office by the Order for misconduct or neglect of duty; but he shall be entitled to a fair trial, and two-thirds of the votes of the representatives present shall be necessary for a removal.

Sec. 2. No officer shall officiate during the time occupied in his trial.

Sec. 3. Any representative may be expelled from his seat as such, for misconduct, upon the vote of two-thirds of the members present at any meeting, after a copy of the resolution of expulsion shall have been served upon him.

ARTICLE VI.

REVENUE.

Sec. 1. The revenue of this Grand Order shall be raised for the purpose of defraying the necessary expenses thereof, and shall be derived from charter fees, donations, and assessments, if necessary of the Subordinate Order.

Sec. 2. The fee for a charter to organize a new Order, with the necessary papers, shall be five dollars, the money to accompany the application.

Sec. 3. All Subordinate Orders failing to be represented in the Grand Order shall pay five dollars for secret work for ensuring year.

Sec. 4. Each Subordinate Order not represented at the annual meeting of the Grand Order, shall be notified of its non attendance by the G.W.S., and if it fail to apply to G.W.P. for the secret work within the year, its charter shall be considered surrendered, and upon proper petition it may be granted a new charter.

ARTICLE VII.

CHARTERS.

Sec. 1. On the written application of twelve or more men of good standing in the community, recommended by the W.P. of the nearest Sub-order asking for a charter to organize a new Order, the Grand Order, or the G.W.P. during the recess, may grant the same, and such Order shall receive its charter and the necessary instruction from the G.W.P., or a member specially deputed; but no Subordinate Order shall be organized with less than seven persons named in the charter, and that no names shall be substituted or added to the original charter members at the time of organizing; all necessary expenses, if any, of the officer or member to be borne by the Order so formed.

Sec. 2. No person but the G.W.P., or his deputy, or the W.P. of a Subordinate Order, is allowed to instruct in the unwritten work, except in the regular meetings of the Order.

Sec. 3. The W.P. of each Subordinate Order shall administer an obligation of secrecy to each member on initiation; said obligation also to be administered by the G.W.P., or his deputy, to all charter members on organization, after the following form:

OBLIGATION.

You [and each of you] do solemnly swear [or affirm] that you make application for membership in Subordinate Order No. ____, A.H.T.A., through pure motives, and that as a member thereof you will keep inviolate and secret all signs and pass-words that are, or should be, kept secret for the good of the Order. That you will not black ball a candidate through personal or political motives. You further promise and swear that you will not cheat, wrong or defraud a member of this Order, or allow any other person to do so if your power to prevent. So help you God.

ARTICLE VIII.

FEES FOR SERVICES.

Sec. 1. The Subordinate Orders shall assist one another in pursuing and prosecuting thieves, and any other service rendered by one Subordinate Order for another, the Order for which said service was performed shall pay a reasonable compensation therefor.

ARTICLE IX.

OFFICERS' FEES.

Sec. 1. The G.W.P., G.W.S., G.W.M., and all deputy G.W.P.'s shall receive one dollar per day for actual service performed in vacation of session and all incidental expenses.

ARTICLE X.

BOOKS, PAPERS, &C.

Sec. 1. All books, papers, and the seal of the Grand Order shall be kept by the G.W.S., and by him turned over to his successor in office. He shall fill all charters.

ARTICLE XI.

STANDING COMMITTEES

Sec. 1. The G.W.P. shall appoint the following committees: A committee on Finance, on Grievance, and on Constitution.

ARTICLE XII.

BLACK BOOK.

Sec. 1. It shall be the duty of each Subordinate Order, to keep a black book, for the purpose of recording the names and residences of all suspicious characters, known criminals, expelled members, and rejected candidates, and each Subordinate Order shall furnish a copy of such person or persons to each subordinate Order in that jurisdiction.

Sec. 2. It shall be the duty of the Worthy Secretary to use all due diligence to ascertain the whereabouts of all suspected persons, rejected candidates and expelled member and report same to the G.W.S. of the Grand Order and he to the G.W.S. of the sister States. But list of rejected candidates shall be published.

ARTICLE XIII.

DESCRIPTION OF STOCK.

Sec. 1. It shall be the duty of all members of Sub Orders to furnish a minute description of all horses and mules owned by them, to the W.S. of their Order.

Sec. 2. It shall be the duty of the W.S. to record all descriptions of stock in a book kept for that purpose.

ARTICLE XIV.

DIMITTED MEMBERS.

Sec. 1. Any member may, by application, dimit from his Subordinate Order, but his or her protection shall cease in said Order from date of said dimit.

Sec. 2. Such dimit shall be granted by a vote of the majority of the members present at a regular meeting of said Sub-Order.

ARTICLE XV.

AMENDMENTS.

Sec. 1. No alteration or amendment to this Constitution, or to the Constitution of Subordinate Orders, shall be made without the concurrence of this Order, and no By Laws shall be adopted by the Subordinate Orders that conflict with the Constitution of the Grand Order or N.O.

ORDER OF BUSINESS FOR G.O.

1. Appointing Committee on Credentials.
2. Report of Committee on Credentials.
3. Reading minutes.
4. Appointment of Committees.
5. Appeals of Subordinate Orders.
6. Report of Officers.
7. Miscellaneous Business.
8. Election of Officers.

FORM OF CREDENTIALS

We herby certify at a regular meeting of Subordinate Order No———, A.H.T.A., held on the ——— Day of ———, 188—, Bro ———, and Bro ——— were chosen delegates to represent said Subordinate Order A.H.T.A., to be held at ———, commencing on the ——— day of ———, 188— Number of members ———

———, W.P.

———, W. Sec.

FORM OF PETITION

We, the following named citizens of ——— Township, ——— County, State of ———, hereby make application to the G.W.P. of ——— for charter to organize a Subordinate Order of the A.H.T.A., to be located at ——— P.O. ——— (signed)
Names.

FORM OF PETITION

To the G.W.P. and members of Subordinate Order No ———, A.H.T.A.: Having a favorable opinion of your Association, I wish to become a member, if found worthy. My age is ——— Years. Occupation ——— Residence ——— I have not been expelled or rejected by any other Order of A.H.T.A.
(Signed)   _____

FORM OF DIMIT

This is to certify that Bro ——— has been a member of Subordinate Order No ———, A.H.T.A., and upon being free from all charges on the books of said order, financially or otherwise.
[Seal.]   (Signed) ————— W.P.

Constitution of Subordinate Order.

ARTICLE I.

OFFICERS.

Sec. 1. The elective officers of a Subordinate Order shall consist of a Worthy President, Worthy Vice President, Worthy Secretary, Worthy Financial Secretary, Worthy Treasurer, Worthy Marshal, and Investigating Committee, who shall be elected annually.

Sec. 2. The Pursuing Committee shall be appointed by the W.P. every six months.

Sec. 3. The above officers may be suspended from office upon charge and proof of malfeasance, by a two thirds vote of the members present at a regular meeting.

Sec. 4. The Subordinate Order shall hold a regular meeting each month.

ARTICLE II.

DUTIES OF OFFICERS.

Sec. 1. It shall be the duty of the W.P. to preside at all meetings and preserve order therein, and give the casting vote in all cases of a tie, except at the election of officers. He shall enforce a due observance of the Constitution of the Grand Order and Subordinate Orders, and shall power to call meetings whenever he shall deem it necessary, draw warrants on the Treasurer for expenses and appropriations as the Order may direct, draw from the treasury money to defray the expenses of the Pursuing Committee without waiting for a vote of the Order. He shall have control of the Pursuing Committee, and when he has received information of the stealing of a horse, or any stealing whatever, from a member of this Order, he shall furnish a description of the stolen property, and of the thief, if known, to the Pursuing Committee, and direct the routes to pursue. He may call as many members of this committee as he thinks necessary.

Sec. 2. The W.V.P. shall preside in the absence of the W.P.

Sec. 3. The W.S. shall make and keep a correct account of the proceedings of the Order at all meetings. He shall conduct the correspondence of the Order.

Sec. 4. The W.F.S. shall keep a correct account with each member of the Order, collect all dues, fees, and other moneys belonging to the Order, and pay them over to the W.T., taking his receipt therefor.

Sec. 5. The W.T. shall receive all moneys from the W.F.S. belonging to the Order, give him his receipt for the same, and pay them out only on the warrant of the W.P. He shall make a correct report every three months of the amount expended since the last report. He shall give bond and security in the sum of two hundred dollars, to be approved by the W.P. and the Order, for a faithful performance of his duty.

Sec. 6. The W.M. shall be present at all meetings of the Order, and carry all messages from the W.P. to other officers and members of the order, also such information as the W.P. or W.S. may direct. He shall, as soon as directed by the W.P., give notice, personally or in writing, of called meetings; he may call as many deputies as he may think necessary; he shall be allowed a reasonable compensation for his services, if faithfully performed.

ARTICLE III.

COMMITTEES.

Sec. 1. The Investigating Committee shall consist of five members of this order. It shall be their duty, when a person or persons have been arrested and handed over to them, charged with stealing or any other violation of the criminal law, to examine the case, and if they find sufficient evidence to found a prosecution, they shall hand the person or persons over to the civil authorities; said committee to attend personally to the prosecution of his or her case, and having the having the means and influence of the Order, they shall have power to call legal advice, if necessary.

Sec. 2. The Pursuing Committee shall consist of two separate and distinct committees, and shall designated as Nos. 1 and 2.

Sec. 3. Committee No. 1 shall consist of two or more members, who shall be appointed by the W.P. It shall be their duty, when directed by the W.P., to hunt in pairs for two days diligently for the trail, but if sooner found, one of the party shall immediately report to the W.P. and the other pursue on the trial.

Sec. 4. The Pursuing Committee No. 2 shall consist of the owner of the stolen property and two other members (and more if necessary), selected by the W.P., whose duty it shall be to pursue the thief after his route is discovered, and as long as any trace of the thief can be found; and if caught, it shall be their duty to hand him over to the Investigating Committee after having said thief or thieves properly arrested with a State's warrant by the owner of the stolen property or the proper prosecuting witness.

ARTICLE IV.

RAISING FUNDS.

Sec. 1. This Order shall have power to levy an ad valorem tax on all personal property of each member, to defray any expenses incurred by any emergency.

ARTICLE V.

APPLICATION FOR MEMBERSHIP.

Sec. 1. Application for membership must be made at a regular meeting; be referred to a committee of three, and lie over one month before being balloted on.

Sec. 2. No Subordinate Order shall act on the petition of the person in the jurisdiction of another Order, without the consent of said Order.

ARTICLE VI.

BALLOTING FOR CANDIDATES.

Sec. 1. All votes for initiation and receiving dimited members shall be by ball ballot, and every member shall vote, except when excused by the W.P.

Sec. 2. No person shall become a member of this Order until he is twenty-one years old, and receives the unanimous vote of all members present at a regular meeting.

Sec. 3. Any candidate having been black balled, and afterwards removing to another locality, it shall be the duty of the W.S. of the Order in which said candidate was black balled to notify by private letter the W.P. of said locality of the fact.

ARTICLE VII.

EXPULSION OF MEMBERS.

Sec. 1. This Order shall have power to exclude any member for crime or conduct unbecoming an Anti, by a two-thirds vote of the members present at a regular meeting. But no member shall be debarred from a fair and impartial trial.

Sec. 2. Any member of the Order divulging any of the secret work or business transactions of the Order, shall, on conviction, be suspended or expelled by a two thirds vote of the order.

ARTICLE VIII.

PROTECTION TO WIDOWS.

Sec. 1. The widow of any member of this Order shall have her property protected the same as her husband would have had, had he lived; and that any Subordinate Order may protect the property of any woman if she will pay the dues and assessments the same as members.

BY-LAWS.

Article 1. The regular meeting of this Order shall be held on or before the moon of each month, at candle lighting.

Art. 2. Any person wishing to become a member of this Order, shall make application to some member thereof, and at the next meeting the vote shall be taken for the admission or rejection of such applicant.

Art. 3. No person shall become a member of this Order until he is twenty-one years old, and receives the unanimous vote of all present at a regular meeting.

Art. 4. Any member who proposes the name of any person for membership, shall inform him of his election or rejection.

Art. 5. No person shall be initiated until his initiation fees are paid.

Art. 6. Any person divulging any transactions of the Order, outside of the Order, shall be fined one dollar and be subject to expulsion.

Art. 7. Each person on becoming a member of this Order shall pay an initiation fee of $1.00.

Art. 8. No person who is not a member of this or a Subordinate Order shall be admitted into our meetings.

Art. 9. It shall be the duty of the President to grant a certificate of membership to any worthy member who desires it.

Art. 10. The President may detail members to do riding or carry orders or messages pertaining to the Order.

Art. 11. No person who has been or may be rejected, shall become a member of this Order until such objection is removed.

Art. 12. Any person giving information that his property has been stolen, and it afterwards appears that it only strayed, the owner shall pay the cost of hunting said property.

Art. 13. Each person serving on detail, or committee, shall receive one dollar per day and have all reasonable expenses paid.

Art. 14. Any member three months in arrears shall be deprived of the benefit of the Order, and six months in arrears, shall be dropped from the roll.

Art. 15. The election of officers shall be held not less than five days nor more than forty days next previous to the meeting of the Grand order.

Art. 16. These By-Laws shall be read at each regular meeting so that no member can plead ignorance of them.

Art. 17. These By-Laws may be altered or amended by the two-thirds vote of the members present, notice having been given in writing, setting forth the proposed amendment, one month previous to the time the vote is to be taken.

The Ladies' Social and Aid
Society *Of The* A.H.T.A. 1909

CONSTITUTION.

PREAMBLE.

We, the mothers, wives, sisters and daughters of the Anti-Horse Thief Association, shall be known as The Ladies' Social and Aid Society of the Anti Horse Thief Association. Organized for the purpose of social entertainment, mentally and morally.

ARTICLE I.

Section 1. The elective officers shall consist of: President, Vice President, Secretary, Treasurer, Marshall, Inside Guard, Chaplain, and an Auditing Committee, which shall consist of three members.

ARTICLE II.

Section 1. Should any vacancy occur by absence of officers at any meeting, the presiding officer shall appoint one to fill vacancy for the evening.

ARTICLE III.

Section 1. It shall be the duty of the President to preside at all meetings and preserve order and give the casting vote in all cases of a tie, except at the election of officers, and applicants for membership. She shall enforce due observance of the Constitution and By-Laws, and shall have power to call meetings when she deems it necessary. Draw warrants on the treasurer for expenses as the order may direct. All orders must be attested by the Secretary.

Sec. 2. The Vice President shall preside in the absence of the President, and assist in the initiation of candidates, and in the absence of both, the Order shall elect a President pro tem.

Sec. 3. The Secretary shall make and keep a correct account of proceedings of the Order at all meetings. She shall conduct the correspondence, attest all orders drawn on the Treasurer, and perform such other duties as the Order may require.

Sec. 4. The Treasurer shall receive all money from the members belonging to the Order, giving her receipt for the same; and pay out only on warrant of the President attested by the Secretary. She shall make a correct report every three months of the amount received and expended since the last report.

Sec. 5. The Marshal shall be present at all meetings of the Order and carry all messages from the President to the officers and members of the Order. She shall, as directed by the President, give notice, personally, or in writing, of called meetings. Also, the Marshal shall take the pass-word and attend the ballot box.

Sec. 6. The Guard shall immediately take charge of the door and shall admit no one without proper signal and Pass Word, unless ordered so by the President.

ARTICLE IV.

Section 1. The auditing Committee shall audit the books of the Treasurer every three months, or as often as the Order deems it necessary.

Sec. 2. The Relief Committee and Visiting Committee shall consist of three members appointed by the President, who shall serve for three months. Their duty shall consist in visiting the sick, helping the distressed, and such other duties as the Order may direct.

Sec. 3. The Entertainment Committee shall consist of three or five. Their duty shall consist of making arrangements for entertainments as the Order may direct, and shall make special effort to suggest entertainments.

ARTICLE V.

Section 1. The Order shall have power to levy a tax by a vote of a majority.

Sec. 2. Applications for membership must be made at regular meetings, be referred to a committee, and lay over to next regular meeting before being balloted upon.

Sec. 3. No person of unclean character shall become a member of this Order.

Sec. 4. Any white lady eighteen years of age and of good moral character shall be eligible to membership, whose father, brother, husband, or son, is a member of the Anti-Horse Thief Association.

Sec. 5. Candidates may be initiated at any regular meeting, or special meeting called for that purpose.

ARTICLE VI.

Section 1. All votes for candidates shall be by ballot, and every member shall vote unless excused by the President.

Sec. 2. Any candidate shall be declared elected who has received a three-fourths majority of all votes cast.

ARTICLE VII.

Section 1. Any person may be expelled for immoral action, or divulging the secrets of this Order to the uninformed.

Sec. 2. No person shall be expelled without a fair and impartial trial.

ARTICLE IX.

Section 1. This Constitution may be amended at any time by three-fourths majority of members present.

BY-LAWS OF THE LADIES' SOCIAL
AND AID SOCIETY OF
THE A.H.T.A.

No. 1. The regular meeting of this Order shall be held where the Order shall direct, and at any time, day or night.

No. 2. Any person wishing to become a member of this Order shall make application through some member thereof, and at the next meeting the vote shall be taken for the admission or rejection of such applicant.

No. 3. Any member who proposes the name of any person for membership shall inform her of her election or rejection.

No. 4. No person shall be initiated until her initiation fees are paid.

No. 5. Each person on becoming a member of this Order shall pay initiation fee of ten cents.

No. 6. The President may detail members for any committee work pertaining to this Order.

No. 7. The dues of each member shall be five cents per quarter in advance.

No. 8. Any member three months in arrears shall stand suspended; but may be re-instated in the same manner as balloting for candidates.

No. 9. The election of officers shall be held one every year at a regular meeting.

No. 10. Where the Constitution and By-Laws are not explicit they shall be governed by parliamentary rules.

No. 11. These By-Laws may be altered by two-thirds vote of the members present, notice having been given in writing setting forth the proposed amendment one meeting previous to the time the vote is to be taken.

No. 12. All elective members shall be voted for by ballot.

No. 13. Ballots for membership shall be by balls, white for election and black for rejection.

No. 14. No person shall be blackballed through any personal or religious motives.

No. 15. There shall not be any personal matters of any kind whatever used in any dealings or entertainments of this Order.

No. 16. At each meeting of this Order it shall be the duty of the President of this Order to read the obligation of both officers and members.

All present when we read and adopt the Constitution and By-Laws shall be considered Charter Members. And each Charter Member shall pay initiation fee same as candidates.

A quorum shall consist of five members.

OBLIGATION OF OFFICERS

I do solemnly pledge my sacred honor, as a member of the Ladies' Social and Aid Society of the A.H.T.A., to perform all the duties of my office, dealing fairly and kindly with all matters brought before me. I will support the Constitution of this Order, and inculcate obedience to all laws, rules and regulations of same. I will not take advantage of my position to bias in any way, either directly, or indirectly, the opinion of any member of this Order, and will do all in my power to promote the interest of same. (Prayer by Chaplain.)

I. I now declare these officers duly installed in their respective positions for the ensuing term.

The Marshal now conducts each to her proper station.

OBLIGATION OF MEMBERS.

I, (name of candidate) do solemnly promise upon my word and honor, to obey the rules and regulations of the Ladies' Social and Aid Society of the Anti-Horse Thief Association.

I furthermore promise that I will do all in my power to assist this organization in entertainment, mentally, and morally. And that I will in no wise reveal any secrets, signs, pass words or grip of this Order, and I will not bring any personal matter into this Order.

ORDER OF BUSINESS.

1. Taking the Pass Word.
2. Roll Call of Officers.
3. Reading of Minutes.
4. Report of Committee of Application.
5. Report of Treasurer.
6. Balloting for Candidates.
7. Initiation of Candidates.
8. Report of Relief and Visiting Committee.
9. Report of Special Committee.
10. Unfinished business.
11. New business.
12. Remarks for the good of the Order.
13. Installation of Officers.
14. Is any member sick or in distress?

Notes

Introduction
1. Nickerson, *The Cambridge Companion to American Crime Fiction*, 3.
2. Szymanski, "Stop Thief! Private Protective Societies in Nineteenth-Century New England," 414.

Chapter 1
1. Hollon, *Frontier Violence*, 17.
2. Nicolosi, "The Rise and Fall of the New Jersey Vigilant Societies," 35.
3. Whitaker and Whitelaw, *The Horse: A Miscellany of Equine Knowledge*, 118.
4. Dunn, *People of the American Frontier*, 19.
5. Volwiler, "Notes and Documents," 393.
6. Ballantine and Ballantine, *The Native Americans*, 197-198.
7. Whitaker and Whitelaw, *The Horse*, 118.
8. Napier, *Kansas and the West*, 4-5.
9. Worobec, "Horse Thieves and Peasant Justice in Post-Emancipation Imperial Russia," 281.
10. Miller, *Why the West Was Wild*, 68.
11. Szymanski, "Stop Thief!" 415.
12. Worobec, "Horse Thieves and Peasant Justice," 283.
13. DuShane, *The Mitchell County Protective Association against Horse Thieves*.
14. Brown, *The Plainsman of the Yellowstone*, 47.
15. Bell, *Reminiscences of a Ranger or, Early Times in Southern California*, 123.
16. Duncan, letter to *Anti-Horse Thief Association Weekly News*.
17. Brown, *The South Carolina Regulators*.
18. Ibid., 29.
19. Szymanski, "Stop Thief!" 414.
20. Ibid., 432.
21. Wilson, "Thunderbolt of the Confederacy, or King of Horse Thieves," 127.
22. Goodrich, *Black Flag: Guerrilla Warfare on the Western Border 1861-1865*, 116.
23. Malin, "Colonel Harvey and His Forty Thieves," 71.

24. Ibid., 72-73.
25. Nolan, *Vigilantes on the Middle Border*, 133.
26. White, "Outlaw Gangs of the Middle Border," 399.
27. Gronert, *Sugar Creek Saga*, 250.

Chapter 2
1. Fleming, *Liberty*, 28.
2. Graves, *Tricks of Rascals*, 3-16, 28-33.
3. Hollon, *Frontier Violence*, 163.
4. Mt. Horeb Area Historical Society, *Mt. Horeb Area Historical Society Pages of the Past.*
5. Graves, *Tricks of Rascals.*
6. Ibid.
7. Friedman, *A History of American Law*, 441.
8. Szymanski, "Stop Thief!" 427-8.
9. Nicolosi, "Rise and Fall of New Jersey Vigilant Societies," 42.
10. Ibid., 43.
11. Higgins, *The Eudora C.P.A. Picnic*, 4.
12. Miller, *Why the West Was Wild*, 285.
13. Szymanski, "Stop Thief!" 419.
14. Herrup, "Law and Morality in Seventeenth-Century England," 115.
15. Harrington, *Hanging Judge*, 64.
16. Ibid., 64-65.
17. Ibid., 79-81
18. Brown, *South Carolina Regulators*, 33.
19. Ibid.
20. Bell, "The United States Army as a Constabulary on the Northern Plains," 23.
21. Bell, *History of Washington County Nebraska*, 38.
22. Wilson, "Thunderbolt of the Confederacy, or King of Horse Thieves," 126.

Chapter 3
1. Brown, *South Carolina Regulators*, 32-33.
2. Klein, "Ordering the Backcountry," 661.
3. Turner, "Western State Making in the Revolutionary Era," 76.
4. Brown, *South Carolina Regulators*, 1.
5. Klein, "Ordering the Backcountry," 673.
6. Brown, *South Carolina Regulators*, 30.
7. Szymanski, "Stop Thief!" 432.
8. Brown, *South Carolina Regulators*, 38.
9. Doniphan County, *Illustrated Doniphan County 1837-1916*, 245.
10. Ibid., 245.
11. Graves, *Tricks of Rascals*, 33.
12. Ogdan, "Letter to Mr. Kenneth Armfield."
13. Consolidated Vigilant Society, *Rules and Regulations to govern the Consolidated Vigilant Society of New Jersey and Pennsylvania*, 4.
14. Brown, *Strain of Violence*, 278.
15. Ibid., 279.

16. Gronert, *Sugar Creek Saga,* 257.
17. Ibid., 430.
18. Anti-Horse Thief Weekly News, "Another Association."
19. Barnsley, *Union Horse Company,* 16.
20. Ibid., 41.
21. Wabash General Association, *Proceedings of the Wabash General Association of Detective Companies,* 11-12.

Chapter 4
1. Brown, *South Carolina Regulators,* 32-33.
2. Klein, "Ordering the Backcountry," 661.
3. Turner, "Western State Making," 76.
4. Brown, *South Carolina Regulators,* 1.
5. Klein, "Ordering the Backcountry," 673.
6. Brown, *South Carolina Regulators,* 30.
7. Szymanski, "Stop, Thief!" 432.
8. Brown, *South Carolina Regulators,* 38.
9. Doniphan County, *Illustrated Doniphan County,* 245.
10. Ibid.
11. Graves, *Tricks of Rascals,* 33.
12. Ogdan, "Letter to Mr. Kenneth Armfield."
13. Consolidated Vigilant Society, *Rules and Regulations,* 4.
14. Brown, *Strain of Violence,* 278.
15. Ibid., 279.
16. Gronert, *Sugar Creek Saga,* 257.
17. Ibid., 430.
18. Anti-Horse Thief Weekly News, "Another Association."
19. Barnsley, *Union Horse Company,* 16.
20. Ibid., 41
21. Wabash General Association, *Proceedings of the Wabash General Association,* 11-12.
22. Culberson, *Vigilantism,* 12.
23. Bell, *Reminiscences of a Ranger,* 23-25.
24. Ibid., 41.
25. Hollon, *Frontier Violence,* 71.
26. Kenyon, "Legal Lore of the Wild West," 682.
27. Holden, "Law and Lawlessness of the Texas Frontier 1875-1890," 202.
28. Kenyon, "Legal Lore of the Wild West," 687.
29. Hamner, *The No-Gun Man of Texas,* 159-160.
30. Kenyon, "Legal Lore of the Wild West," 695.
31. Holden, "Law and Lawlessness," 199.
32. Gard, *Frontier Justice,* 211.
33. Ibid., 212.
34. Holden, "Law and Lawlessness," 198.
35. Cook, *Hands Up! Or, Twenty Years Detective Life in the Mountains and on the Plains,* 204-5.
36. Miller, *Why the West Was Wild,* 172.
37. Brown, *Plainsman of the Yellowstone,* 398.

38. Ibid., 399
39. Fleharty, *Death on the Western Frontier,* 156-157.
40. Holden, "Law and Lawlessness," 197.
41. Ibid., 198.
42. Greenberg, *Citizens Defending America,* 487.
43. Howard, *Montana,* 127-28; 134.
44. Miller, *Why the West Was Wild,* 55. Emphasis in the original.
45. Ibid., 56-57.
46. Alley, *The Violent Years,* 42.
47. Ibid., 43.
48. Ibid., 45.
49. Ibid., 48.
50. Culberson, *Vigilantism,* 2.

Chapter 5
1. Griffith, *Outlaw Tales of Nebraska* 34.
2. Durham, *The Negro Cowboys,* 181.
3. Ibid., 186.
4. Ibid., 186
5. Smarsh, *Outlaw Tales of Kansas,* 66.
6. Miller, *Why the West Was Wild,* 342.
7. Hoy, *Flint Hills Cowboys,* 272-275.
8. Miller, *Why the West Was Wild,* 343.
9. Ibid., 373.
10. Griffith, *Outlaw Tales of Nebraska,* 53.
11. Durham, *The Negro Cowboys,* 177.
12. Wall, *How Kentucky Became Southern,* 46.
13. Ibid., 46-50.
14. Wilson, "Thunderbolt of the Confederacy," 120.
15. Ibid., 125.
16. Cook, *Hands Up!,* 29-30.
17. Brantner, *Durand Once Had Reputation as "Hanging Town."*
18. YesterYear Once More, "Archive for the 'Horse Thief Thursday' Category."
19. Harrington, *Hanging Judge,* 93-95.
20. Dary, *True Tales of the Old-Time Plains,* 104-106.
21. YesterYear Once More, "Horse Thief Thursday."
22. Ibid., 2010.
23. Brown, *South Carolina Regulators,* 32.

Chapter 6
1. Miller, *Why the West Was Wild,* 451.
2. Ibid., 452.
3. Ibid., 51, 55.
4. Ibid., 46.
5. Alley, *The Violent Years,* 41.
6. Cook, *Hands Up!,* 1.
7. Miller, *Why the West Was Wild,* 148.
8. Ibid., 345.

9. History Channel, "Andrew Jackson Kills Charles Dickinson in Duel."

10. Gurr, *Violence in America,* 38.

11. Ibid., 38.

12. Roosevelt, *Ranch Life and the Hunting-Trail,* 120.

13. Ibid., 128.

14. Traub, "Rewards, Bounty Hunting, and Criminal Justice in the West," 298.

15. Ibid.

16. Nelson, *The Cowman's Southwest,* 170.

17. Hamner, *No-Gun Man of Texas,*153-154.

18. White, "Outlaw Gangs of the Middle Border,"401.

19. Harrington, *Hanging Judge,* 148.

20. Coe, *Frontier Doctor,* 139.

21. Ibid., 146-147.

Chapter 7

1. Nicolosi, "Rise and Fall of the New Jersey Vigilant Societies," 35.

2. *Anti-Horse Thief Association Weekly News* 1902, 1.

3. Nolan, *Vigilantes on the Middle Border,* 128-129.

4. Nicolosi, "Rise and Fall of the New Jersey Vigilant Societies," 37.

5. Ibid.

6. Gresham, *The Story of Major David McKee Founder of the Anti-Horse Thief Association,*14-15.

7. Nolan, *Vigilantes on the Middle Border,* 132-133.

8. Gresham, *Story of Major David McKee,* 17.

9. Ibid., 18.

10. The A.H.T.A. Weekly News, "Joined Hands to Fight Crime," 1.

11. Nolan, *Vigilantes on the Middle Border,* 134.

12. Gresham, *Story of Major David McKee,* 32.

13. Brush Valley Association for the Detection and Apprehension of Horse Thieves, *Constitution and By Laws,* 2.

14. Scottville Horse Thief Detecting Society, *Constitution and By Laws of the Scottville Horse Thief Detecting Society,* 2.

15. Gresham, *Story of Major David McKee,* 36-37.

16. Graves, *Law for Criminal Catchers,* 12.

17. Grand Order of the Anti-Horse Thief Association, *Constitution of the Grand and Subordinate Orders of the A.H.T.A. of Missouri,* 13.

18. C.P.A., *Constitution and By-Laws of the C.P.A. Olathe Horse League Number Eighty-Nine,* 12.

19. Kansas Collection, Salina Public Library.

20. Nolan, *Vigilantes on the Middle Border,* 140.

21. Christian County Historical Society, *Christian County Historical Society Millennium Milestones: County History to 2000.*

22. Chetopa Democrat, "Horsethief Captured," 2.

23. Nolan, *Vigilantes on the Middle Border,* 141 and Gresham, *Story of Major David McKee,* 74.

24. Gresham, *Story of Major David McKee,* 39.

25. Ibid., 30-31.

26. Szymanski, "Stop, Thief!" 423.
27. Howard, *Montana*, 126-36.
28. Burdick, *Tales from Buffalo Land: The Story of George "W" Newton*, 20.
29. Ibid., 22.
30. White, "Outlaw Gangs of the Middle Border," 388.
31. *Anti-Horse Thief Weekly News*, "Joined Hands to Fight Crime," 1902, 1.
32. Corson, "G.W.P. Address," 5.
33. *Johnson v. Miller et al.*
34. *Anti-Horse Thief Weekly News*, "The Anti-Horse Theif Society Fifty Years Ago," 15.
35. Juhnke, "Mob Violence and Kansas Mennonites in 1918."

Chapter 8
1. Anti-Horse Thief Association, *Proceedings of the Second Annual Meeting of the Anti-Horse Thief Association, held at Emporia*, 5-6.
2. The letter is from B.B. Chapman and written on October 31, 1973. The document (call # K 352.2; An 87; Pam v 2; No. 1 & 2) is titled Black List 1901. It contains eight numbered pages and has no publisher data printed.
3. Oklahoma Anti-Horse Thief Association, *Black List*, 1901, 1-8.
4. Connor, "Official C.P.A. Notice," 2.
5. Howard, "Owner Found by Aid of the News," 1.
6. Graves, *Tricks of Rascals*, 2.
7. Nolan, *Vigilantes on the Middle Border*, 136.
8. *Anti-Horse Thief Weekly News*, 1902, 1.
9. Graves, *The Anti-Horse Thief Association: Its Origin and Principles*, 18-19.
10. Ladies Auxiliary of The Anti-Horse Thief Association, *Ladies Auxiliary of the Anti-Horse Thief Association*, 3.
11. Traub, "Rewards, Bounty Hunting, and Criminal Justice in the West," 292.
12. Gresham, *The Story of Major David McKee*, 59. Emphasis added.
13. Stark, "Excerpts from the Past," 3.
14. *J.P. Crawford v. George W. Ferguson, County Judge.*
15. *State of Iowa v. C.J. Van Hoozer.*
16. *The State v. Wilkins Taylor.*
17. *State of Kansas v. Maurice E. Waterman.*
18. Gresham, *Story of Major David McKee*, 75.
19. Rammelkamp, "Edward Beecher—Abolitionism—Illinois College," 201.
20. Eagle Creek Marion Co. Horse Thief Detecting Company, *Constitution of the Eagle Creek Marion Co. Horse Thief Detecting Company*, 4.
21. Jackson, *Ku Klux Klan in the City 1915-1930*, 145.
22. Ibid., 145-46.

23. Sims, *The Klan, 2nd Edition*, 287.
24. Ibid., 286.
25. Ibid.
26. Jackson, *Ku Klux Klan*, 167.
27. Sims, *The Klan, 2nd Edition*, 163.
28. Gresham, *Story of Major David McKee,* 76.
29. Hanan, "Report from the Grand Worthy President," 6.
30. Lapham, "State President's Annual Report," 11.
31. Anti-Theft News, "Danger Ahead."

Appendix 1
1. These are based on primary documents viewed. I have seen references of many other such societies in the states listed. Societies without names that explicitly mention horse theft are listed if detection and apprehension of horse thieves were stated as a priority in their constitution/by-laws. An example would be Cooper Vigilance Society, whose charter includes authorization under "An act to amend an act entitled An act to authorize the formation of companies for the detection and apprehension of horse thieves and other felons and defining their powers."
2. This was a body that brought together the various anti-horse thief societies within the state of Indiana.

Appendix 2
1. This document is in the possession of the author and is missing the complete By-Laws section. Publisher: Greenfield, ILL. Argus, Book and Job Printing Establishment. 1883.

Bibliography

Alley, J. Mark. *The Violent Years: The Founding of a Kansas Town.* Hillsboro, KS: Multi Business Press, 1992.

Allman, Mark. *Who Would Jesus Kill? War, Peace, and the Christian Tradition.* Winona, MN: St. Mary's Press, 2008.

Andrews, Charles M. *The Colonial Period of American History: The Settlements*, vol 1. New Haven: Yale University Press, 1934.

———. *The Colonial Period of American History: The Settlements*, vol 2. New Haven: Yale University Press, 1936.

"Anti Horse Thief Collection - File." *Notes of Sub-Order No. 281 Anti-Thief Association.* Kansas Collection, Salina Public Library.

Anti-Horse Thief Weekly News. "Another Association." 2, no. 2 (February 12, 1903): 1.

———. "Battled with Horse Thieves in Oklahoma." 1, no. 22 (July 3, 1902).

———. "Brief Historical Sketch." (July 31, 1902).

———. "Joined Hands to Fight Crime." 1, no. 11 (November 13, 1902): 1.

———. "Not a Vigilance Committee." (July 31, 1902).

———. "The Anti-Horse Thief Society Fifty Years Ago." 9, no. 8 (March 24, 1910): 15.

Anti-Horse Thief Association. *Anti-Horse Thief Association Ritual.* 1905. http://www.stichtingargus.nl/vrijmetselarij/ahta_r.html.

———. *Anti-Horse Thief Association* 1, no. 16 (May 22, 1902).

———. *Proceedings of the Second Annual Meeting of the Anti-Horse Thief Association held at Emporia, Kansas October 17, 1883.* Emporia: G.H. Rowland & Co's Print, 1884.

Anti-Horse Thief Association Weekly News. "Aim and Object of the A.H.T.A." (May 8, 1902): 2.

———. "Early History of the Order." (May 15, 1902).

Anti-Horse Thief Weekly News. (September 11, 1902): 2.

———. "A Hot Chase." (July 3, 1902): 1.

———. "Pool Murderers to Hang." (July 24, 1902): 1.

———. "Whitecaps Blown to Fragments." 1, no. 23 (July 10, 1902): 3.

———. "Missouri." 12, no. 5 (March 6, 1913): 4.

———. "Watch Your Legislature." 12, no. 5 (March 6, 1913): 2.

———. "Horse Thieves Busy." 12, no. 6 (March 13, 1913): 5.

———. *Anti-Horse Thief Weekly News* 13, no. 11 (April 23, 1914): 4.

———. "A.H.T.A. Prepares to Initiate Bill." *Anti-Horse Thief Weekly News* 13, no. 6 (March 19, 1914): 1.

———. *Anti-Horse Thief Weekly News* 2, no. 1 (Feb 5, 1903): 4.

———. "Antis in Arkansas." 1, no. 28 (August 14, 1902).

Anti-Thief Association News "Dog Owners form Anti-Thief Group." July 1940: 1.

Anti-Theft News. "Danger Ahead." 36, no. 6 (October 1940): 1.

Ballantine, Betty, and Ian Ballantine, eds. *The Native Americans: An Illustrated History.* New York: Turner Publishing, 1993.

Barnsley, Edward, ed. *Union Horse Company.* Doylestown, PA: Doylestown Printing Shop, 1951.

Bell, John T. *History of Washington County Nebraska: Its Early Settlement and Present Status, Resources, Advantages and Future Prospects.* Omaha: Herald Steam Book and Job Printing House, 1876.

Bell, Larry D. "The United States Army as a Constabulary on the Northern Plains." *Great Plains Quarterly* 13, no. 1 (1993): 21-32.

Bell, Major Horace. *Reminscences of a Ranger or, Early Times in Southern California.* Los Angeles: Farnell, Caystile & Mathes, Printers, 1881.

Brantner, Joey and Louise Miller. "Durand Once Had Reputation As 'Hanging Town.'" St. Paul Pioneer Press, 1963. http://web.durand.k12.wi.us/hs/history/COLEMAN/HANGING.HTM.

Brown, M. *The Plainsman of the Yellowstone.* New York: G.P. Putnam's Sons, 1961.

Brown, Richard D. "The Emergence of Urban Society in Rural Massachusetts, 1760-1820." *Journal of American History* (1974): 29-51.

Brown, Richard Maxwell. *Strain of Violence: Historical Studies of American Violence and Vigilantism.* New York: Oxford University Press, 1975.

———. *The South Carolina Regulators.* Cambridge: Belknap Press of Harvard University Press, 1963.

Brush Valley Association for the Detection and Apprehension of Horse Thieves. *Constitution and By Laws.* Logansville, PA: Henry Held, Printer, 1853.

Burdick, Usher L. *Tales From Buffalo Land: The Story of George "W" Newton (Old-Time Buffalo Hunter of Dakota and Montana).* 2nd ed. Baltimore: Wirth Brothers, 1939.

Central Protection Agency. *Constitution and By-Laws of the C.P.A. Olathe Horse League Number Eighty-Nine.* Olathe, KS: Olathe Mirror Print, 1911.

Cahalan, Margaret Werner. *Historical Corrections in the United States, 1850-1984 (NCJ-102529).* Rockville, MD: US Department of Justice, Bureau of Justice Statistics, 1986.

Papers of the War Department 1784 to 1800. Center for History and New Media. George Mason University. http://wardepartmentpapers.org.

Charles H. Marsh v. The Wells Fargo Company Express. 88 Kansas 538; 129 P. 168; 1913 Kansas (Supreme Court of Kansas, January 11, 1913).

Cherryvale (KS) Republican. "Untitled." *Anti-Horse Thief Weekly News* 8, no. 1 (February 4, 1909): 7.

"Horsethief Captured." *Anti-Horse Thief Weekly News* 1, no. 4 (Feb 27, 1902): 1. Originally published in the *Chetopa Democrat.*

Christian County Historical Society. *Christian County Historical Society*

Millennium Milestones: County History to 2000. Taylorville, IL: Christian County Genealogical Society, 2000.

Coe, Urling. *Frontier Doctor: Observations on Central Oregon and the Changing West.* Corvallis, OR: Oregon State University Press, 1996.

Coldham, Peter Wilson. *The King's Passengers to Maryland and Virgina.* Westminster, MD: Family Line Publications, 1997.

Connor, W.S. "Official C.P.A. Notice." *Anti Horse Thief Weekly News* 1, no. 48 (1903): 1.

Consolidated Vigilant Society. *Rules and Regulations to govern the Consolidated Vigilant Society of New Jersey and Pennsylvania.* Newton, PA: Enterprise Print, 1913.

Cook, David J. *Hands Up! Or, Twenty Years Detective Life in the Mountains and on the Plains.* Santa Barbara: The Narrative Press, 2001.

Corson, E. "G.W.P. Address." *Proceedings of the Fourth Annual Session of the Kansas Grand Order of the Anti Horse Thief Association.* Address at Kansas Grand Order of the Anti Horse Thief Association, Girard, Kansas. 1886.

Cory, C.E. "Passing of the Horsethief." *Mail and Breeze Topeka,* July 28, 1899, 1.

Croft, M.L. "Insurance Against Thieves." *Anti-Horse Thief Weekly News* 1, no. 4 (February 27, 1902): 3.

Crown. "Untitled." *Anti-Horse Thief Weekly News* 1, no. 16 (May 22, 1902): 2.

Culberson, William C. *Vigilantism: Political History of Private Power in America.* Westport, CT: Praeger Publishers, 1990.

Dallmeyer, Diane. *Chesterfield Observer.* June 10, 2009. http://www.chesterfieldobserver.com/news/2009-06-10/family/026.html.

Dary, David. *True Tales of the Old-Time Plains.* New York: Crown Publishers, 1979.

Dent, Anthony. *The Horse Through Fifty Centuries of Civiilzation.* New York: Rinehart and Winston, 1974.

Dimsdale, Thomas J. *The Vigilantes of Montana, Or Popular Justice in the Rocky Mountains.* 1866. Reprint, New York: Time-Life Books, 1981.

Doniphan County. *Illustrated Doniphan County 1837-1916.* Troy, KS: Trojan Graphics, 1999.

Duncan, J.E. "Indians Make Good Antis." *Anti-Horse Thief Weekly News* 1, no. 11 (April 17, 1902).

Dunn, Walter S. *People of the American Frontier: The Coming of the American Revolution.* Westport, CT: Praeger Publishers, 2005.

Durham, Philip and Everett L. Jones. *The Negro Cowboys.* New York: Dodd, Meade and Company, 1965.

DuShane, Neil, transc. *The Mitchell County Protective Association against Horse Thieves.* 2002. http://iagenweb.org/mitchell/localdat/horsethi.htm.

Eagle Creek Marion County Horse Thief Detecting Company. *Constitution of the Eagle Creek Marion CO. Horse Thief Detecting Company.* Indianapolis: Ellis & Spann Printers, 1850.

Earle, Alice Morse. *Curious Punishments of Bygone Days.* Chicago: Herbert S. Stone & Company, 1896.

Edwards, Elwyn Hartley. *The Encyclopedia of the Horse.* New York: DK Publishing, 1994.

Ekirch, A. Roger. "Bound for America: A Profile of British Convicts

Transported to the Colonies, 1718-1775." *William and Mary Quarterly,* 3d ser., 42, no. 2 (April 1985) : 184-200.

Ekirch, A. Roger. "The Transportation of Scottish Criminals to America during the Eighteenth Century." *Journal of British Studies* 24, no. 3 (1985): 366-374.

Fleharty, Eugene D. and Gary K. Hulett. *Death on the Western Frontier: Kansas, 1875-1879.* Manhattan, KS: Sunflower University Press, 2000.

Fleming, Thomas. *Liberty: The American Revolution.* New York: Viking Press, 1997.

Frantz, Joe. "The Frontier Tradition: Invitation to Violence." In *Violence in America: Historical and Comparative Perspectives*, edited by Hugh Davis Graham and Ted Robert Gurr, 127-54. New York: Signet, 1969.

Friedman, Lawrence M. *A History of American Law: 3rd Edition.* New York: Simon & Schuster, 2005.

Gard, Wayne. *Frontier Justice.* Norman: University of Oklahoma Press, 1949.

Gaskins, R. "Changes in the Criminal Law in Eighteenth-Century Connecticut." *American Journal of Legal History*, 1981: 309-42.

Goodrich, Thomas. *Black Flag: Guerrilla Warfare on the Western Border 1861-1865.* Bloomington: Indiana University Press, 1995.

Graham, Hugh Davis and Ted Robert Gurr, eds. *Violence in America: Historical and Comparative Perspectives.* New York: Signet, 1969.

Grand Order of the Anti-Horse Thief Association. *Constitution of the Grand and Subordinate Orders of the A.H.T.A. of Missouri.* Palmyra, MO: Herald Print, 1887.

Graves, W.W. *Graves' Manual.* St. Paul, KS: A.J. Hopkins Publications, 1927.

———. *Law for Criminal Catchers.* St. Paul, KS: Press of the Anti-Horse Thief Association Weekly News, 1906.

———. *The Anti-Horse Thief Association: Its Origin and Principles.* St. Paul, KS: The News, 1914.

———. *Tricks of Rascals.* St. Paul, KS: Press of the Anti-Horse Thief Association Weekly News, 1905.

———., ed. "Pioneer Horse Thieves." In *Anti-Horse Thief Weekly News* 1, no. 19 (June 12, 1902). St. Paul, Kansas: St. Paul Press, 1902.

Greenberg, Martin Alan. *Citizens Defending America: From Colonial Times to the Age of Terrorism.* Pittsburgh: University of Pittsburgh Press, 2005.

Greenberg, Milton. "Loyalty Oaths: An Appraisal of the Legal Issues." *Journal of Politics* 20, no. 3 (1958): 487-514.

Gresham, Hugh Cleveland. *The Story of Major David McKee Founder of the Anti-Horse Thief Association.* Cheney, Kansas: 1937.

Griffith, T.D. *Outlaw Tales of Nebraska.* Guilford, CT: TwoDot, 2010.

Gronert, Ted. *Sugar Creek Saga: A History and Development of Montgomery County.* Crawfordsville, IN: Wabash College, 1958.

Gurr, Robert Ted. *Violence in America.* Vol 2, *Protest, Rebellion, Reform.* Thousand Oaks, CA: Sage, 1989.

Haines, Francis. "The Northward Spread of Horses Among the Plains Indians." *American Anthropologist, New Series* 40, no. 3 (1938): 429-437.

Hamner, Laura. *The No-Gun Man of Texas: A Century of Achievement.* Amarillo, TX: 1935.

Hanan. "Report from the Grand Worthy President." *Proceedings of the*

Second Annual Meeting of the Anti-Horse Thief Association, 5-6. Emporia, KS: G.H. Rowland & Co.'s Print, 1884.

Harrington, Fred Harvey. *Hanging Judge*. 1951, reprinted Norman: University of Oklahoma Press, 1995.

Herrup, Cynthia B. "Law and Morality in Seventeenth-Century England." *Past & Present* 106, no. 1 (1985): 102-123.

Higgins, Cindy. *The Eudora C.P.A. Picnic*. Eudora, KS: Eudora Area Historical Society, 1997.

Hilgenberg, James F. and William M. Oliver. *A History of Crime and Criminal Justice in America*. Columbus: Allyn & Bacon, 2006.

History Channel, The. *Andrew Jackson kills Charles Dickinson in duel*. 2011. http://www.history.com/this-day-in-history/andrew-jackson-kills-charles-dickinson-in-duel.

Hoig, Stan. *Tribal Wars of the Southern Plains*. Norman: University of Oklahoma Press, 1993.

Holden, W.C. "Law and Lawlessness on the Texas Frontier 1875-1890." *Southwestern Historical Quarterly* 44, no. 2 (1940): 188-203.

Hollon, W. Eugene. *Frontier Violence: Another Look*. New York: Oxford University Press, 1974.

Howard, Joseph K. *Montana: High, Wide, and Handsome*. New Haven: Yale University Press, 1943.

Howard, J.W. "Owner Found by Aid of the News." *Anti-Horse Thief Weekly News* 1, no. 48 (1903): 1.

Hoy, Jim. *Flint Hills Cowboys: Tales of the Tallgrass Prairie*. Lawrence: University Press of Kansas, 2006.

Illinois Anti-Horse Thief Association. *Journal of Proceedings and State Constitution and By-Laws*. Taylorville: Daily Courier Company, 1922.

Ingalls, Sheffield. *History of Atchison County Kansas*. Lawrence, KS: Standard Publishing, 1916.

J.P. Crawford v. George W. Ferguson, County Judge. A-1096 5 Okla. Crim. 377; 115 P. 278; 1911 Okla. Crim App. (Court of Criminal Appeals of Oklahoma, May 2, 1911).

Jackson, Kenneth T. *Ku Klux Klan in the City 1915-1930*. New York: Oxford University Press, 1967.

Johnson v. Miller et al. 63 Iowa 529; 17 N.W. 34; 1884 Iowa Sup. (Supreme Court of Iowa, April 25, 1884).

Juhnke, James. "Mob Violence and Kansas Mennonites in 1918." *Kansas Historical Quarterly* 43, no. 3 (1977): 334-350.

Kammer, Sean M. "Public Opinion is More than Law: Popular Sovereignty and Vigilantism in the Nebraska Territory." *Great Plains Quarterly* 31, no. 4 (2011): 309-324.

Kansas Anti-Horse Thief Association. *Proceedings of the Forty-First Annual Session Held at Caldwell, Kansas, October 18 & 19 1922*. St. Paul, Kansas: Press of The News, 1922.

———. *Proceedings of the Second Annual Meeting of the Anti-Horse Thief Association, held at Emporia, Kansas October 17, 1883, Emporia, Kansas*. Emporia: G.H. Rowland & Co.'s Print, 1884.

———. *Proceedings of the Thirty-Ninth Annual Session Held at Salina, Kansas*. St. Paul, Kansas: Press of The News, 1922.

Kansas Division of the Anti-Horse Thief Association. *The Anti-Horse Thief Association Proceedings of the Thirty-Sixth Annual Session of the Kansas Division.* St. Paul, Kansas: Press of the Anti-Horse Thief Assocation News, 1917.

Kansas Grand Order of the Anti-Horse Thief Association. *Proceedings of the Fourth Annual Session of the Kansas Grand Order of the Anti-Horse Thief Association.* Girard, Kansas: Girard Press Job Rooms, 1886.

Kenyon, Carleton W. "Legal Lore of the Wild West: A Bibliographical Essay." *California Law Review* 56, no. 3 (1968): 681-700.

Klein, Rachel N. "Ordering the Backcountry: The South Carolina Regulaion." *William and Mary Quarterly*, 1981: 661-680.

Kowalewski, David. "Vigilantism." In *International Handbook of Violence Research*, edited by Wilhelm Heitmeyer and John Hagan. Netherlands: Kluwer Academic Publishers, 2003: 339-49.

Ladies Auxiliary of The Anti-Horse Thief Association. *Ladies Auxiliary of The Anti-Horse Thief Association.* 1916.

Lapham, John. "State President's Annual Report." In *Anti-Horse Thief Association Proceedings: Thirty-Ninth Annual Session, Kansas Division*, by Kansas Anti Horse Thief Association. St. Paul, Kansas: Press of the News, 1920.

Little, C. and C. Shefield. "Frontiers and Criminal Justice: English Private Prosecution Societies and American Vigilantism in the Eighteenth and Nineteenth Centuries." *American Sociological Review*, (1983): 796-808.

Macionis, John J. *Society: The Basics, 9th Edition.* Upper Saddle River, NJ: Pearson Prentice Hall, 2007.

Malin, James C. "Colonel Harvey and His Forty Thieves." *Mississippi Valley Historical Review* 19, no. 1 (1932): 57-75.

Maloney, W.S. "Teaches Biblical Doctrine." *Anti-Horse Thief Weekly News* 1, no. 34 (September 25, 1902): 1.

McMaster, J.B. "The President's Address Delivered at the AHA Annual Meeeting in Washington, D.C." *American Historical Review*, 1906: 515-528.

Mechem, Kirke, ed. *Annals of Kansas 1886-1925.* Vol 1, *1886-1910.* Topeka: Kansas State Historical Society, 1954.

———. *Annals of Kansas 1886-1925.* Vol 2, *1911-1925.* Topeka: Kansas State Historical Society, 1956.

Miller, Nyle H. and Joseph W. Snell. *Why the West Was Wild: A Contemporary Look at the Antics of Some Highly Publicized Kansas Cowtown Personalities.* Topeka: Kansas State Historical Society, 1963.

Moriarty, Laura J. and Barbara Peat. *Assessing Criminal Justice/ Criminology Education: A Resource Handbook for Educators and Administrators.* Durham: Carolina Academic Press, 2009.

Mt. Horeb Area Historical Society. *Mt. Horeb Area Historical Society Pages of the Past.* December 12, 2005. http://www.mounthorebhistory. org.

Napier, Rita. *Kansas and the West: New Perspectives.* Lawrence: University Press of Kansas, 2003.

Nelson, Oliver. *The Cowman's Southwest: Being the Reminiscences of Oliver Nelson.* Glendale: A.H. Clark Company, 1953.

Neosho County Republican. "A Nest of Horse Thieves Routed: One Killed and One Arrested on Suspicion." September 24, 1885: 4.

New York Times. "Horse-Stealing as an Art." November 15, 1902.

Newton Reliance Company. *History Newton Reliance Company.* 2009. http://newtownreliance.org/history.htm.

Nickerson, Catherine Ross, ed. *The Cambridge Companion to American Crime Fiction.* Cambridge: Cambridge University Press, 2010.

Nicolosi, A. "The Rise and Fall of the New Jersey Vigilant Societies." *New Jersey History,* 1968: 29-53.

Nolan, Patrick B. *Vigilantes on the Middle Border: A Study of Self-Appointed Law Enforcement in the States of the Upper Mississippi from 1840 to 1880.* New York: Garland Publishing, Inc., 1987.

Ogdan, Ray. Letter to Mr. Kenneth Armfield, August 7, 1947. *Eudora Area Historical Society C.P.A. Archive Holdings.* August 7, 1947.

Oklahoma Anti-Horse Thief Association. *Black List.* Unknown: 1901.

Owen, J.S., annalist. *Annals of Kansas 1886-1925.* Vol 1. Edited by K. Mechem. Topeka: Kansas State Historical Society, 1954.

Parker, William B. "Another Kindred Association." *Anti-Horse Thief Weekly News* 1, no. 44 (December 1, 1902): 3.

Peek, James R. "Missouri." *Anti-Horse Thief Weekly News* 12, no. 5 (March 6, 1913): 4.

Pershing, John J. "Organize for Self Protection." *Anti-Thief Association News,* September 1935: 1.

Pfeifer, Michael J. *Rough Justice: Lynching and American Society, 1874-1947.* Urbana: University of Illionois Press, 2004.

"A Power in the Land." *Anti-Thief Association News,* October 1940: 3. Previously published in *Pittsburg (Kansas) Headlight.*

Powell, Lew. *North Carolina Miscellany.* April 30, 2011. http://www.lib.unc.edu/blogs/ncm/index.php/2011/04/30/horse-thieves-werent-easily-discouraged/.

Rammelkamp, Charles. "Edward Beecher - Abolitionism - Illinois College." In *Transactions of the Illinios State Historical Society for the Year 1908,* by Illinois State Historical Society, 199-203. Springfield: Illinois State Journal Company, 1909.

Roosevelt, T. *Ranch Life and the Hunting-Trail.* New York: The Century Company, 1888.

Rousseau, Jean-Jacques. *On The Social Contract,* 1762. Reprint, Mineola, NY: Dover Publications, Inc., 2003.

Russell, George B. *Hoofprints in Time.* South Brunswick: Barnes & Co., 1966.

Ruston, Peter and Gwenda Morgan. *Rogues, thieves and the rule of law.* Bristol, PA: University College London, 1998.

Scottville Horse Thief Detecting Society. *Constitution and By-Laws of the Scottville Horse Thief Detecting Society.* Greenfield, IL: Argus Book and Job Printing Establishment, 1883.

Shaprio, Fred R. *The Oxford Dictionary of American Legal Quotations.* New York: Oxford University Press, 1993.

Sheffield, Christopher P. and Craig B. Little. "Frontiers and Criminal Justice: English Private Prosecution Societies and American Vigilantism in the Eighteenth and Nineteenth Centuries." *American Sociological Review* 48, no. 6 (1983): 796-808.

Sims, Patsy. *The Klan, 2nd Edition.* Lexington: University Press of Kentucky, 1996.

Smarsh, Sara. *Outlaw Tales of Kansas.* Guilford, CT: Morris Book Publishing, LLC, 2010.

Smith, W.H. "Notes from W.H. Smith Grand Secretary." In *The Anti-Horse Thief Weekly News Feb. 12, 1903* 2, no. 2, 1. St. Paul, Kansas: St. Paul Press, 1903.
Stark, Judi. "Excerpts from the Past." *Kansas Quarterly Interest*, 2001.
State of Iowa v. C.J. Van Hoozer. 192 Iowa 818; 185 N.W. 588; Iowa Sup. (Supreme Court of Iowa, December 13, 1921).
State of Kansas v. Maurice E. Waterman. No. 14,914 75 Kan. 253; 88 P. 1074; 1907 Kan. (Supreme Court of Kansas, February 9, 1907).
State v. Wilkins Taylor. No. 28742 320 Mo. 417; 8 S.W.2d 29; 1928 Mo (Supreme Court of Missouri, June 21, 1928).
Stevenson, Burton. *The Home Book of Proverbs, Maxims and Familiar Phrases.* New York: Macmillan Company, 1948.
Szymanski, A. "Stop, Thief! Private Protective Societies in Nineteenth-Century New England." *New England Quarterly*, 2005: 407-439.
Traub, S. "Rewards, Bounty Hunting, and Criminal Justice in the West: 1865-1900." *Western Historical Quarterly* 19, no. 3 (1988): 287-301.
Trelease, Allen W. *White Terror: The Ku Klux Klan Conspiracy and Southern Reconstruction.* New York: Harper & Row, 1971.
Turner, Frederick Jackson. "Western State Making in the Revolutionary Era." *The American Historical Review*, 1895: 70-87.
U.S. Government. "The Colonial Period: Culture and Society in the 13 British Colonies." In *Outline of US History*, edited by George Clack. April 2008. http://www.america.gov/st/educ-english/2008/April/200804 07112617eaifas0.4646417.html.
Volwiler, A.T. "Notes and Documents: WIlliam Trent's Journal at Fort Pitt, 1763." *Mississippi Valley Historical Review* 11, (1924): 390-413.
Wabash General Association. *Proceedings of the Wabash General Association of Detective Companies 20th Annual Session.* Danville, IL: Commercial Company, Steam Printers, 1880.
Wall, Maryjean. *How Kentucky Became Southern: A Tale of Outlaws, Horse Thieves, Gamblers, and Breeders.* Lexington: University Press of Kentucky, 2010.
Webb, Eli. "Urges Action Against Anti-American Activities." *Anti-Thief Association News*, July 1940: 1.
Welch, Michael. *Corrections: A Critical Approach Second Edition.* New York: McGraw Hill, 2004.
White, Richard. "Outlaw Gangs of the Middle Border: American Social Bandits." *The Western Quarterly* 12, no. 4 (1981): 381-408.
Whitaker, Julie and Ian Whitelaw. *The Horse: A Miscellany of Equine Knowledge.* New York: Thomas Dunne, 2007.
Wilson, W. "Thunderbolt of the Confederacy, or King of Horse Thieves." *Indiana Magazine of History* 54, no. 2 (1958): 119-130.
Press Publishing Company (New York World). *The World 1914 Almanac and Encyclopedia.* New York: Press Publishing, 1913.
Worobec, Christine D. "Horse Thieves and Peasant Justice in Post-Emancipation Imperial Russia." *Journal of Social History* 21, no. 2 (1987): 281-293.
YesterYear Once More. "Archive for the 'Horse Thief Thursday' Category." February 6, 2009. http://yesteryearsnews.wordpress.com/category/ horse-thief-thursday/page/2/.
———. *Posts tagged "Horse Thieves."* July 22, 2010. http:// yesteryearsnews.wordpress.com/tag/horse-thieves/.

Index